YUM-O!

the family cookbook

rachael ray
YUM-O!
the family cookbook

clarkson potter/publishers
new york

www.crownpublishing.com

www.clarksonpotter.com

Clarkson N. Potter is a trademark and Potter and colophon are registered trademarks of

Random House, Inc.

Library of Congress Cataloging-in-Publication Data

is available upon request

ISBN 978-0-307-40726-9

Printed in the United States of America

Design by Jennifer K. Beal

10 9 8 7 6 5 4 3 2 1

First Edition

About
yum-o!

The Yum-o! organization empowers kids and their families to develop healthy relationships with food and cooking by teaching families to cook, by feeding hungry kids, and by funding cooking education.

For more information, check out www.yum-o.org.

Contents

introduction

I've written lots of cookbooks, so what makes this one different? The goal of *Yum-o! The Family Cookbook* is to make eating healthier as a family easier, more affordable, and fun. Think of it as a playbook on how to fit more grains, veggies, and whole foods into your family's overall game plan. I've always said that food that's good for you can be just as cool and delish as food that is not so good for you. The trick is finding recipes that everyone will love and that are full of healthy ingredients. The good news is it's easier than you think.

Start by thinking about what your family already likes to eat. Macaroni and cheese out of a box with powdered orange sauce may taste good, but it's not giving your body a whole lot to work with. Real macaroni and cheese, prepared with whole-wheat pasta and a combination of chicken stock, whole milk, and sharp farm-fresh cheese is even more delish and will give your body super-powers! Our section on Lunch Boxes That Rock and Snack-Attackers is full of recipes that are way cooler than those prepackaged lunches you can get in the grocery store. If you want your kids to be real individuals at the lunch table check out the Bento Box recipes on page 51 and fill a thermos with Meatball and Orzo Soup (page 58) or Chicken Taco Soup (page 60)

It's all part of a new way of thinking about food, and making better choices about what we eat, cook, and serve our families, and I'm not the only one who's on the case. Former President Bill Clinton and the Clinton Foundation, along with the American Heart Association, started the Alliance for a Healthier Generation. The goal is to help kids, their schools, and their families make better choices in their eating habits both at school and at home so we can all become a healthier nation. Type 2 diabetes is on the rise among children, but by changing up the foods we eat a little we can get a hold on this disease.

When we launched the Yum-o! organization President Clinton joined us for a taping of our show. (So cool!) He was really honest about his own struggles with eating too much of the wrong kinds of foods, like the supertasty fast foods that can be super bad for our bodies if we eat them too often. He really inspired me to make this my mission: get kids and parents healthier by giving them fun and affordable recipes that are easy to make so the whole family can eat well and eat together as often as possible

Best of all, the recipes in this book are designed to get the whole family in the kitchen—not just around the dinner table. Cooking is cool because it's all about sharing, so try sharing some time in the kitchen. You don't need to be a fancy chef or the chief of chopping to make any of these recipes. Picky eaters—grown-ups or little kids—are a lot less picky when they take part in the making of a meal. With supervision, even young children can help by grating cheese and peeling carrots or measuring any kind of ingredients, and they love to brag about how they helped make the meal (see suggestions throughout the book for tasks the itty bitties can help with). Older kids can make the recipes all by themselves because most of them are supersimple.

You'll notice we don't list nutritional breakdowns on these recipes because I believe if you eat well you can eat more and also because when I cook, I don't measure. I have always measured everything in my hand or by "eyeballing" the amount. Most of these recipes are probably higher in fiber and lower in fat than what you're cooking now, but they are not strictly "low-fat" recipes. As I always say, it's all about moderation. We all deserve an indulgent pancake breakfast with plenty of maple syrup, or a cheesy-good baked pasta once in a while, and as long as it's not an everyday thing, no problem! If you or someone in your family needs to follow a specific diet, share the book with your doc and let him or her pick and choose the recipes that will work best for you. My hope is that these recipes will help us all become healthy enough that we never need to go on extreme diets of any kind.

Throughout this book you'll find not only my recipes but also some of yours as well! Families have been submitting these Kids 2 Kids recipes to our website and we've chosen a few we thought you (and the young cooks in your family) would enjoy. If you're into cooking and want to share some of your recipes, check out yum-o.org.

a note to kids

Welcome to the Yum-o! community!

The mission of Yum-o! is to empower kids and their families to develop healthy relationships with food and cooking. That means that every day, we are teaching kids and their families to cook, working to help feed kids who don't have enough to eat, and helping kids who want to learn more about food in school. We want to see a country where everyone can experience the joys of food and cooking.

You're an important part of the Yum-o! community. At www.yum-o.org, we are building a place where kids and their parents are talking and learning about food and cooking—a community that is continually growing and changing, thanks to your participation. On the website you can find all kinds of fun things to do and learn. In "Recipes," you can look up super-easy and healthy recipes from me—and people like you! We've got hundreds of recipes that you can choose based on your age and skill level. Under "Get Inspired," you'll find loads of stories about other kids who love to cook in the Your Stories section. That's where kids and parents share their favorite recipes and nuggets of wisdom from the kitchen. If you want to get involved and help your community, go to "How Cool Is That?" where we highlight people and organizations that are making a difference in our world. You can read these stories and get inspired to do something in your neighborhood or school, too!

We hope that you'll stop by the site and contribute your favorite cooking stories, tips, and recipes, and that you'll let us know what you're up to in your community and at school when it comes to food so that other kids can learn from you. And we hope that you'll spread the word, too! You can start by printing out our seasonal "Kitchen Road Map" to hang up in your kitchen and pass it around at school or at other gatherings. It's got tips and recipes all ready to go! We've also got food trivia, printables, and more. I bet you are one smart cookie!

Thank you for being a part of Yum-o! Now, let's get cooking!
Rach and the Yum-o! Team

START A "FAMILY GOOD FOOD FUND"

The totals at the market check-out lines can be scary these days. Lean meats and fresh produce are just too expensive to be included in many family food budgets. I think it's the foods that are processed, dyed with colors, and mixed up with chemicals that should cost more: look at all the work that goes into them! The stuff that just grows should be cheap, right? Wrong.

Still, be prepared to buy better food when it goes on sale by starting up a Family Good Food Fund. Keep a jar by the front door and every night when you come in the door, drop in your spare change. Once a month, tally it up and trade it in, using the food fund to stock up when the price is right. Keep your eyes peeled for the occasional sale on lean meats and vegetables. Stock up on chicken tenders or boneless, skinless breasts; sirloin steak; or pork loin chops or tenderloins. Portion out the meats and freeze them so you can cook with them whenever you want.

Veggies freeze well, too. Packaged frozen veggies are fine, but your own homemade broccoli spears will have even better flavor and be bigger than those in ten-ounce boxes. To freeze most any veggie, cut them in serving-size pieces and blanch for two minutes in boiling salted water. Drain, and pack in heavy-duty plastic food storage bags. When you are ready to use, defrost, drain, and cook as you like, from steaming to stir-frying.

With smart shopping and the help of a secret slush fund, you can afford to eat good food that is good for you every day.

Rise and Dine!

By now just about everybody knows that breakfast is the most important meal of the day—and not just for kids! Even grown-ups will get through their mornings with better concentration (and smiles on their faces) when they start the day with one of these healthy, substantial meals under their belt. Sugary cereal? No way when there's a breakfast-burrito-to-go on the counter, or a batch of creamy oatmeal all packaged up to take along to the office just waiting in the fridge. Breakfast sammies from the drive-through take a backseat to the super-size, super-healthy breakfast sammies you can make at home. Even favorites like flapjacks and bagel-with-a-schmear become guiltless pleasures when they come topped with fruit or veggie spreads. And don't forget that breakfast is a prime time for getting more whole grains onto the menu—in your pancakes, waffles, even English muffins. **It's never too early to start eating right!**

MENU

Apple Flapjacks

Better Pancakes

Eggs Florentine Get
  Wacky with Waffles

Peanut Butter and Jelly
  French Toast

Monkey Spread French Toast

Bunny Spread

Asian Veggie Spread

BLT Spread

Raisin-Walnut Spread

Bird-in-a-Bagel

Farmer's Bagel Baskets

Super-size Healthy Breakfast
  Sandwiches

Bottom-of-the-Box Breakfast
  Sundae

"Instant" Oatmeal, Master
  Recipe: The Classic

Banana Nut Oatmeal

Apple Cinnamon Oatmeal

Health Nut Oatmeal

Tortilla Scrambles

Brocco-Cheese Burritos

Spinach-Feta Mediterranean
  Burritos

Apple Flapjacks

- 8 medium McIntosh apples, peeled, cored, and diced
- ¾ cup apple cider
- 1 cinnamon stick
- ¾ cup pure maple syrup
- Nonstick cooking spray (as needed)
- Buckwheat pancake mix (enough to make 8 pancakes, prepared according to package directions)

THE ITTY BITTIES CAN:

- peel apples
- mix pancake batter

Preheat the oven to 150°F.

Combine the apples and cider in a medium sauce pot. Add the cinnamon stick and cook until the apples break down and become a chunky sauce, 12 to 15 minutes. Stir in the maple syrup and reserve over low heat.

While the apples are simmering, preheat a griddle or large nonstick skillet and coat with cooking spray. Mix up the pancake batter and make 8 pancakes, keeping the finished pancakes warm in the oven.

When the pancakes are ready to serve, remove the cinnamon stick from the sauce and layer 2 flapjacks with lots of homemade apple-maple sauce on each plate. Yum-o!

SERVES 4

Better Pancakes

My friend Mollie makes these pancakes for her two girls, three-year-old twins Isabel and Maya. The girls are great eaters, but even the best eaters demand pancakes between breakfasts of scrambles, yogurt, fruit, or oatmeal. Mollie's solution for giving her girls the food they need to start their day and giving them what they want (which is pancakes) is to ignore the directions on the back of the box. Where it says add one egg, she adds more; where it says add water she adds milk, bumping up the proteins. In addition, she stirs in plenty of fresh fruits for fiber. Good idea, Mol; thanks for sharing!

FOR PANCAKE MIXES REQUIRING LIQUID AND EGG, USE

- 2 cups **mix**
- 1 cup **milk**, plus more as needed
- 3 **eggs**

FOR PANCAKE MIXES REQUIRING LIQUID **ONLY**, USE

- 2 cups **mix**
- 1½ cups **milk**, plus more as needed
- 2 **eggs**

FRUIT STIR-INS

- ½ pint **blueberries**
- ½ **banana**, cut in half lengthwise, then sliced

  Canola oil, for the griddle
  Maple syrup or honey, for serving

> **THE ITTY BITTIES CAN:**
> - measure ingredients
> - slice banana
> - mix batter

In a mixing bowl, combine the pancake mix, milk, and eggs. Stir and add more milk as needed until you achieve a consistency that is thick but pourable. Add the blueberries and sliced bananas and stir to combine.

Preheat a large nonstick skillet over medium heat. Add a drizzle of canola oil and when it shimmers, pour in ¼ cup of batter for each pancake. Cook until the sides are dry and bubbles are popping around the edges, then flip the pancakes and cook the other side. Continue until all the batter is used up. Serve with maple syrup or honey.

SERVES 4; MAKES ABOUT 12 PANCAKES

pancake tacos with fruit salsa

KID 2 KID

SUBMITTED BY BASIMA AND DAUGHTER LAILA (AGE ELEVEN)
FROM LAGUNA NIGUEL, CALIFORNIA

1 cup blueberries • 1 cup sliced strawberries • 1 cup blackberries • 1 cup sliced kiwi • 1 cup raspberries • 1 box whole-wheat pancake mix plus any additional ingredients needed to make the pancake batter • Vanilla yogurt or syrup, for serving (optional)

Mix the blueberries, strawberries, blackberries, kiwi, and raspberries in a medium bowl and set aside.

Prepare the pancake batter according to the package directions, making enough for 10 to 12 pancakes. Preheat a large nonstick griddle or skillet. Make one extra-large pancake, cooking until golden on each side. Place ½ cup of "fruit salsa" in the center of the pancake and top with a dollop of yogurt or a drizzle of syrup. Fold like a taco and serve. Repeat with the remaining batter and fruit salsa.

SERVES 4 TO 6

Eggs Florentine Get Wacky with Waffles

What a fancy-pants way to start the day!

INGREDIENTS

2 tablespoons EVOO (extra-virgin olive oil)
2 tablespoons butter
½ small onion, chopped
1 garlic clove, grated or finely chopped
Salt and freshly ground black pepper
1 (10-ounce) box frozen chopped spinach, defrosted and excess water squeezed out in a kitchen towel
Freshly grated nutmeg
1 tablespoon all-purpose flour
½ cup milk
½ cup chicken stock
4 frozen whole-grain waffles
4 slices Canadian bacon
8 eggs
Hot sauce (optional)
1 vine-ripe tomato, cut in 4 slices
1 cup grated Gruyère or other Swiss cheese

> **THE ITTY BITTIES CAN:**
>
> - squeeze spinach dry
> - grate nutmeg and cheese
> - beat eggs

INSTRUCTIONS

Preheat the broiler to high. Set the rack in the second slot from the top.

In a medium skillet, heat 1 tablespoon of the EVOO, once around the pan, and 1 tablespoon of the butter over medium-high heat. Once the butter has melted, add the onions and garlic and season with a little salt and pepper. Cook, stirring every now and then, for 2 to 3 minutes or until the onions start to get tender. Add the spinach and season with a little nutmeg and stir to combine. Sprinkle the spinach mixture with the flour and cook, stirring, for 1 minute. Add the milk and chicken stock and bring up to a bubble. Simmer the mixture until thick, 3 to 4 minutes, then cover and keep warm off the heat.

While the spinach mixture is cooking, toast up your frozen waffles.

Place a large nonstick skillet over medium-high heat with the remaining tablespoon of EVOO. Add the Canadian bacon and cook on each side for 1 to 2 minutes, until

lightly browned. Transfer to a plate and cover to keep warm. Return the skillet to medium-low heat and add the remaining tablespoon of butter. While the butter melts, beat the eggs with a splash of water, some salt and pepper, and a couple dashes of hot sauce, if you like. Add the eggs to the skillet and scramble to your preferred doneness.

To serve, place a slice of the Canadian bacon on top of each toasted whole-grain waffle. Top with some of the spinach mixture, then eggs, a tomato slice, and cheese. Slide under the broiler for a couple of minutes to melt the cheese.

SERVES 4

Peanut Butter and Jelly French Toast

INGREDIENTS

- 8 slices whole-grain bread
- 4 tablespoons peanut butter, creamy or chunky
- 4 tablespoons all-fruit spread, flavor of your choice
- 6 eggs
- ½ cup milk
- 2 teaspoons pure vanilla extract
- 4 tablespoons (½ stick) butter
- ½ cup pure maple syrup, warm

> **THE ITTY BITTIEſ CAN:**
> - spread PB&J onto bread
> - beat egg batter

INSTRUCTIONS

Spread 4 slices of the bread with peanut butter and the other 4 with jelly to make four PB&J sammies. Beat the eggs, milk, and vanilla together in a bowl.

Place a large nonstick skillet over medium heat and add 2 tablespoons of the butter. When the butter is almost melted, dunk two of the sammies into the egg batter and let the excess drip off. Place in the pan. Fry the sammies until golden brown on both sides, 3 to 4 minutes per side. Repeat with the remaining 2 sammies. Cut the French toast sammies into 4 sticks apiece and serve with warm maple syrup.

SERVES 4

Monkey Spread French Toast

- 1 small ripe **banana**, peeled and sliced
- 1 tablespoon **honey**, plus some for drizzling
- ¼ cup **peanut butter**
- 4 slices **whole-grain bread**
- 1 tablespoon **butter**
- 2 **eggs**, beaten
- A splash of **milk**

THE ITTY BITTIES CAN:

- mash banana
- measure ingredients
- spread monkey spread onto bread

INSTRUCTIONS

In a small bowl, mash the banana with a fork. Stir in the honey and peanut butter.

Use the monkey spread to make 2 sandwiches on the whole-grain bread. Melt the butter in a large nonstick skillet. Stir the beaten eggs and milk together in another bowl, dip the sandwiches in the egg mixture, and cook in the butter until golden on each side. Drizzle with a little extra honey and serve.

SERVES 2 MONKEYS

fabulous french toast

SUBMITTED BY CONNIE M. AND HER DAUGHTER AVERY
(AGE NINE) FROM MACOMB, MICHIGAN

One night, after watching a segment of *$40 a Day* in which Rachael ate French toast at an East Coast diner, Avery handed her mom a list of ingredients and informed her that she wanted to make her own version that weekend. Here it is:

3 eggs • ½ cup milk • 1 teaspoon ground cinnamon • ¼ teaspoon freshly grated or ground nutmeg • 1 teaspoon pure vanilla extract • Nonstick cooking spray • ½ loaf French bread cut in thick slices • 1 to 2 tablespoons butter • 3 tablespoons brown sugar • 1 cup walnuts • ½ cup ricotta cheese • ½ cup sliced strawberries • ½ cup diced cantaloupe • ½ cup halved red grapes • Confectioners' sugar

Preheat a griddle or large nonstick skillet. Preheat the oven to 200°F.

In a shallow dish, beat together the eggs, milk, cinnamon, nutmeg, and vanilla. Spray the skillet or griddle with cooking spray. Working in batches, dip the slices of bread in the egg mixture, let the excess drip off, then place in the skillet and cook for 3 minutes per side, or until golden brown. Place on a baking sheet in the low oven to keep warm while you cook the rest of the French toast slices.

In a separate skillet, cook the butter and the brown sugar together until the butter is melted. Add the walnuts and toss to coat with the mixture. Cook for 3 to 4 minutes, or until the sugar is dissolved and the walnuts are fragrant. Stir the mixture into the ricotta cheese.

Spread a thin layer of ricotta on half the French toast slices and top with another piece to make a sandwich. Top with fruit and a sprinkle of confectioners' sugar.

SERVES 4

SPREAD IT! YOU'LL LIKE IT!

Plain cream cheese? What a bore! Stir it up and bump up the fiber and vitamins in your toast toppers. Spread any of these mix-ins on toasted whole-wheat or whole-grain English muffins, toast, or bagels. The spreads will keep for a couple of days in the fridge.

TIDBIT
Here's a bagel tip for you . . .
You know how some bagels are gi-normous? If you are serving them up as a toast alternative, use a serrated knife to cut them into three horizontal slices rather than just splitting them in half; eat 2 slices at a time and save the third for bagel chips or another day.

Bunny Spread

All the rabbits in your house will love this, even the veggie reluctant!

- ½ cup shredded carrots (store-bought is fine)
- 1 celery rib, finely chopped
- 3 tablespoons finely chopped salad olives with pimiento
- 2 scallions, green and white parts, finely chopped
- 8 ounces low-fat or regular cream cheese, at room temperature

INSTRUCTIONS

In a bowl, combine all of the ingredients and mix thoroughly.

SERVES 4

> **THE ITTY BITTIES CAN:**
> - shred carrots
> - mix spread

Asian Veggie Spread

INGREDIENTS

- 3 scallions, green and white parts, finely sliced
- ¼ seedless cucumber, finely chopped
- 1 tablespoon tamari or soy sauce
- 8 ounces low-fat or regular cream cheese, at room temperature

INSTRUCTIONS

In a bowl, combine all of the ingredients and mix thoroughly.

SERVES 4

> **THE ITTY BITTIES CAN:**
> - measure ingredients
> - chop cucumber
> - mix spread

BLT Spread

A drizzle of EVOO (extra-virgin olive oil)

4 slices turkey bacon, finely chopped

1 small leek, white and tender green parts, quartered lengthwise, chopped, rinsed, and dried

Pinch of salt

Freshly ground black pepper

8 ounces low-fat or regular cream cheese, at room temperature

1 plum tomato, seeded and finely chopped

> ## THE ITTY BITTIES CAN:
> - chop bacon
> - wash leeks
> - seed tomato
> - mix spread

INSTRUCTIONS

Place a small skillet over medium heat with a drizzle of EVOO. Once the skillet is hot add the chopped bacon and cook, stirring frequently, for 3 to 4 minutes or until the bacon is crispy. Drain off any excess fat. Add the leeks, season with a pinch of salt and black pepper to taste, and cook until the leeks are tender, 2 to 3 minutes.

Cool the bacon and leeks in a bowl for 1 minute, combine with the cream cheese, then fold in the tomatoes.

SERVES 4

Raisin-Walnut Spread

- ½ cup golden or dark **raisins**
- ½ cup **walnut pieces**
  Pinch of **salt**
- ½ teaspoon **ground cinnamon**
- 8 ounces low-fat or regular **cream cheese** or peanut butter, at room temperature

> THE ITTY BITTIES CAN:
>
> - chop walnuts
> - drain raisins
> - mix spread

INSTRUCTIONS

Place the raisins in a bowl and pour enough boiling water over them to just cover. Let them sit and plump up while you toast the nuts. Place a small dry skillet over medium heat; add the walnuts and toast, shaking the pan frequently, until they are golden, 5 to 6 minutes.

Drain the raisins well, return them to the bowl, and add the toasted walnuts, a pinch of salt, and the cinnamon. Mix thoroughly with the cream cheese or peanut butter.

SERVES 4

Bird-in-a-Bagel

- ½ **apple**, your favorite variety, finely chopped
- 1 cup shredded **sharp Cheddar cheese**
- 4 slices **Canadian bacon**, cut in half and then into thin strips
  Salt and **freshly ground black pepper**
- 1 tablespoon **butter**
- 2 **whole-wheat bagels**, split
- 4 **eggs**

> ### THE ITTY BITTIES CAN:
> - chop apple
> - shred cheese
> - cut Canadian bacon into strips
> - beat eggs

In a bowl combine the chopped apple, shredded Cheddar, and Canadian bacon. Season with salt and pepper.

Place a large nonstick skillet over medium-high heat and add the butter. When the butter is melted, add the bagels to the skillet, cut side down. Carefully crack one egg into each of the bagel holes. Place a piece of foil or a lid on the skillet and cook for 3 to 4 minutes, or until the eggs have firmed up enough for you to flip the bagels over. Flip gently to avoid breaking the egg yolks. Once flipped, top each bagel with some of the apple mixture, cover the skillet with foil or a lid again, and cook the bird-in-a-bagel until the cheese melts, 2 to 3 minutes more.

Slide a bagel onto each plate and eat up!

SERVES 4

fruit freezies

SUBMITTED BY CHERYL S. AND HER DAUGHTER AMBER
(AGE SEVEN) FROM FOLSOM, CALIFORNIA

KID 2 KID

8 ounces Key lime yogurt • ⅓ cup frozen blueberries

In a medium bowl, stir the yogurt until it is smooth. Fold in the blueberries. Spoon the mixture into Popsicle molds or small paper cups and insert the sticks (or Popsicle sticks if using the cups). Freeze for 2 hours or until firm.

MAKES 4 POPSICLES

Farmer's Bagel Baskets

It's not every day that you get to say a *half* is better than a *whole,* but that's the case when you're eating in moderation. If you want, you can use 4 whole eggs and 4 egg whites.

- 1 small **potato**
- 2 **whole-wheat bagels**
- 1 tablespoon **EVOO** (extra-virgin olive oil)
- ½ small **onion**, finely chopped
- ½ **green bell pepper**, seeded and chopped
- 4 slices **Canadian bacon**, chopped
  Salt and **freshly ground black pepper**
- 1 **plum tomato**, seeded and chopped
- 8 **eggs**, beaten with a splash of water
- 1 cup sliced or shredded **extra-sharp Cheddar cheese**

> ### THE ITTY BITTIES CAN:
>
> - poke potato
> - peel and chop cooled potato
> - pull guts out of bagels
> - chop bacon
> - seed bell pepper and tomato

INSTRUCTIONS

Poke the potato in a few places with a fork and microwave for 5 to 6 minutes, or until tender. When it is cool enough to handle, peel and chop the potato.

Preheat the broiler and place a rack in the center of the oven. (You can also use a toaster oven.)

Slice the bagels horizontally and use your fingers to remove the guts from each of the four halves, making them into bagel baskets. Place the bagels under the broiler or in the toaster oven to toast until golden, 2 to 3 minutes. Remove and reserve.

While the bagels are toasting, preheat a medium nonstick skillet over medium-high heat with the EVOO, once around the pan. Add the onions, bell peppers, and Canadian bacon and cook, stirring every now and then, for 2 to 3 minutes or until the onions start to get tender. Add the chopped potato and salt and pepper to taste, cook for about a minute more, then add the chopped tomatoes. Stir to combine, then add the beaten eggs. Scramble the eggs but keep them a little on the loose side. Fill the bagel baskets with the eggs, top with the cheese, and slide back under the broiler to melt the cheese.

SERVES 4 FARMERS OR THEIR KIDS

eggs in a nest with sheets, blankets, and pillows

SUBMITTED BY STACY M. AND LAYNE
(AGE FIVE) FROM PIKETON, OHIO

KID 2 KID

1 tablespoon softened butter • 1 slice whole-wheat bread • 1 large egg, beaten • 1 slice ham or turkey • 1 slice Provolone cheese

Heat a nonstick skillet over medium heat. Spread half of the butter on one side of the bread slice. Use a cookie cutter to cut out the middle of the bread slice, leaving ½ inch around the opening. Save the cut-out part for the "pillow."

Add the remaining butter to the skillet. When it is melted, place the bread and "pillow" in the skillet, butter side up. When they are golden brown, flip both with a spatula. Carefully pour the egg into the hole and cook until almost set, stirring a little to allow uncooked egg to come in contact with the skillet. Place the ham "sheet" on the bread slice and top with the cheese "blanket." Cover the skillet until the cheese has melted, 1 to 2 minutes. Remove the lid and serve. Don't forget the pillow!

SERVES 1

Super-size Healthy Breakfast Sandwiches

The folks at the drive-through windows are always trying to get you to supersize your order for an extra nickel. Sure, it seems like a bargain, but in the end, all those "food bargains" end up supersizing *us*! If you have a BIG appetite, this is a tasty, healthy way to go. It's a meal that will keep you going—and keep you in the same size jeans. Open wide!

INGREDIENTS

- 2 tablespoons EVOO (extra-virgin olive oil)
- 1 pound ground chicken or ground turkey breast
- ¼ cup pure maple syrup
- 1 tablespoon poultry seasoning
- Salt and freshly ground black pepper
- 8 egg whites or whole eggs, your choice
- ¼ cup milk or reduced-fat milk
- 1 or 2 dashes of hot sauce (optional)
- 1 scallion, finely chopped
- 4 sandwich-size whole-wheat English muffins
- 1 cup shredded sharp Cheddar cheese

> **THE ITTY BITTIES CAN:**
> - shape sandwich patties
> - beat eggs
> - shred cheese

OPTIONAL TOPPERS

Thinly sliced apple
Tomato slices
Sliced dill pickles

INSTRUCTIONS

Preheat the broiler. (You can also make this in a toaster oven.)

Preheat a large nonstick skillet over medium heat with 1 tablespoon of the EVOO, once around the pan.

In a mixing bowl, combine the ground chicken or turkey, maple syrup, poultry seasoning, salt, and pepper. Form 4 large, thin patties and cook for 10 to 12 minutes, turning once. Remove and reserve. Add the remaining tablespoon of EVOO to the skillet. Beat the egg whites or eggs with milk, salt and pepper, hot sauce, and chopped scallion. Pop the split English muffins under the broiler to toast when you add the eggs to the skillet. Scramble the eggs until they are done to your taste, and remove the muffins from the oven when nicely browned (don't forget them!).

Top each muffin bottom with a sausage patty, one fourth of the eggs, and ¼ cup of the cheese. Place the sammies without their tops under the broiler for 1 minute to melt the cheese. Top with sliced apple, tomato, or pickle if you like, or just set the tops in place and serve.

SERVES 4

Bottom-of-the-Box Breakfast Sundae

INGREDIENTS

- ½ cup **berries** of your choice
- ½ cup **vanilla yogurt**
- ¼ cup **cereal** from the bottom of a box, such as cornflakes or crisped rice

THE ITTY BITTIES CAN:

- build sundaes

INSTRUCTIONS

Layer the ingredients into a glass or parfait dish beginning with the berries, then the yogurt, and then the cereal. Repeat two more times to finish with a layer of cereal on top.

SERVES 1

super strawberry smoothies

KID 2 KID

SUBMITTED BY LAURA S. AND HER SON TIM
(AGE FOURTEEN) FROM MANITOWOC, WISCONSIN

1 cup skim milk • 1 banana • 6 strawberries, hulled • 4 ounces low-fat strawberry yogurt

Combine the milk, banana, strawberries, and yogurt in a blender. Pulse until smooth.

SERVES 2

"INSTANT" OATMEAL

Dollar for dollar, oatmeal is the best food value around when it comes to breakfast. It's a whole grain, it can be jazzed up in tons of different ways, and if you buy it from the bulk bins it costs just pennies per serving. Choose old-fashioned rolled oats (not instant) for the most fiber and nutrients, and make it up in big batches to reheat throughout the week. You can either portion it out into small containers to grab and go in the morning, or just reheat a scoop at a time in the microwave for a virtually instant breakfast.

Master Recipe

INGREDIENTS

- 3 cups old-fashioned (not instant) oatmeal
- 3 cups skim milk, plus more for serving
- ½ cup brown sugar
- ½ cup dried dates, chopped
- ½ cup currants or raisins
- ½ teaspoon salt

INSTRUCTIONS

Combine the oatmeal, milk, and 4 cups water in a large, deep saucepan and bring to a boil over medium-high heat. When it boils, quickly turn the heat down to very low. Stir in the brown sugar, dried fruits, and salt and cook at a low simmer for 15 to 20 minutes, or until very thick and creamy. Stir often to prevent the bottom from scorching.

Serve with additional milk, or cool and refrigerate to reheat later in the week.

SERVES 8

NOW TRY . . .
Banana Nut Oatmeal

S W A P

½ cup **pure maple syrup** for the brown sugar

2 **bananas**, chopped, for the dried fruit

A D D

¾ cup **toasted walnut pieces**, chopped

I N S T R U C T I O N S

Follow the directions for the original recipe, stirring in the chopped nuts just before serving the oatmeal. Top with additional milk if desired.

> THE ITTY
> BITTIES CAN:
>
> • chop bananas and walnuts

OR TRY . . .
Apple Cinnamon Oatmeal

S W A P

2 **Granny Smith apples**, peeled, cored, and chopped, for the dried fruit

A D D

2 teaspoons **ground cinnamon**, plus more for serving

I N S T R U C T I O N S

Follow the directions as for the original recipe, adding the cinnamon along with the apples. Serve with additional milk and a sprinkle of cinnamon.

> THE ITTY
> BITTIES CAN:
>
> • peel and chop apples

AND TRY . . .
Health Nut Oatmeal

SWAP:

½ cup **honey** for the brown sugar

1 cup **Craisins** (dried cranberries) for the dates and currants

THE ITTY
BITTIES CAN:

• measure
  ingredients

ADD

¼ cup **flaxseed meal**

½ cup toasted, **unsalted sunflower seeds**

½ cup **Grape-Nuts cereal**

INSTRUCTIONS

Follow the directions for the original recipe, stirring in the flaxseed meal and sunflower seeds along with the Craisins. Serve with additional milk and sprinkle with a tablespoon of the Grape-Nuts cereal if desired.

Tortilla Scrambles

Chips 'n' salsa for breakfast? It can be good *and* good for you; check it out.

- 2 cups lightly crushed yellow, blue, or whole-grain tortilla chips
- 2 tablespoons canola oil
- 6 eggs, lightly beaten
  Freshly ground black pepper
- 1 cup grated sharp Cheddar, Monterey Jack, or pepper Jack cheese
- 1 cup tomato or tomatillo salsa or 2 plum tomatoes, seeded and chopped

> THE ITTY BITTIES CAN:
> - crush chips
> - beat eggs
> - grate cheese

INSTRUCTIONS

Place the crushed tortilla chips in a bowl and add boiling water to just barely cover. Let them sit until the chips are soft, a couple of minutes. Drain the chips thoroughly.

Heat the oil in a large nonstick skillet over medium-high heat. Season the beaten eggs with some black pepper, then add the softened tortilla chips and stir to combine. Add the egg mixture to the skillet along with the cheese, stir to combine, and let it start to brown up on one side. Break up the egg mixture into 4 wedges and flip each wedge to brown the second side, just a couple of minutes.

Transfer the eggs to serving plates and top each wedge with salsa or lots of chopped tomatoes.

SERVES 4

Brocco-Cheese Burritos

BREAKFAST
TO-GO
BURRITOS

Hit the road with
one of these babies
and you can go
for hours!

INGREDIENTS

2 tablespoons **EVOO** (extra-virgin olive oil), twice
around the pan
1 (10-ounce) box **frozen chopped broccoli**, defrosted
and squeezed dry, or a couple of large stalks
of broccoli, trimmed, florets and stalks finely
chopped
8 **eggs** or 4 whole eggs and 4 egg whites
Splash of **milk**
Salt and **freshly ground black pepper**
4 large **whole-wheat flour tortillas**
1 cup shredded **sharp Cheddar cheese**

THE ITTY
BITTIES CAN:

• trim and chop
broccoli
• shred cheese

INSTRUCTIONS

Heat the EVOO in a large nonstick skillet over medium-high heat. Once the skillet
is hot, add the defrosted broccoli and cook for 2 minutes. (If using fresh broccoli,
cook, stirring every now and then, until the broccoli is lightly browned, 5 to
6 minutes.)

Beat the eggs with a splash of milk and season with salt and pepper. Add the eggs
to the skillet and scramble with the broccoli. Remove from the heat.

While the broccoli and eggs cook, heat the tortillas in a dry skillet over medium-
high heat until blistered and soft, 1 minute on each side.

Make burritos by placing one quarter of the hot eggs on one side of each tortilla.
Top with one quarter of the cheese, tuck in the sides, then wrap and roll. Wrap
each burrito in foil and go.

SERVES 4

Spinach-Feta Mediterranean Burritos

- 2 tablespoons **EVOO** (extra-virgin olive oil), twice around the pan
- 1 (10-ounce) box **frozen chopped spinach**, defrosted and squeezed dry in a kitchen towel
- ¼ cup **sun-dried tomatoes**, chopped (optional)
- 8 **eggs** or 4 whole eggs and 4 egg whites, beaten with a splash of water
  Salt and **freshly ground black pepper**
- 4 **whole-wheat flour tortillas**
- 1 cup **feta cheese crumbles**

> ### THE ITTY BITTIES CAN:
> - squeeze the spinach dry
> - beat eggs
> - crumble feta cheese

INSTRUCTIONS

Heat the EVOO in a large nonstick skillet over medium-high heat. Once the oil is hot, add the defrosted spinach and the sun-dried tomatoes, if using, and heat through.

Season the eggs with salt and pepper and add to the pan with the spinach. Cook until the eggs are softly scrambled. Remove from the heat.

While the eggs cook, heat the tortillas in a dry skillet over medium-high heat until blistered and soft, 1 minute on each side.

Make burritos by placing one quarter of the hot egg mixture on one side of each tortilla. Top with one quarter of the feta cheese, tuck in the sides, and wrap and roll. Wrap each burrito in foil and go.

SERVES 4

rise and dine!

Lunch Boxes That Rock and Snack-Attackers

Of all the meals we eat, lunch is the one most likely to be eaten away from home, whether at school, work, or just on the go. That doesn't necessarily have to equal a routine of PB&Js and fast food, though; I've got a list of lunch box stuffers so delish there will be no swapping going on at your kids' lunch table! Fill a thermos with hearty soup, make lunch a dip-fest with dunkable meat and veggies cut in bite-size pieces, or pack a bento box–style container of "sushi" treats and even the lunch ladies will be green with envy!

Snacking can be the downfall of kids of all ages— chips, fries, and anything salty are my weaknesses—so I've included lots of healthier options for snack attacks without hitting the vending machines or loading up on sugary or fat-laden munchies. And check out the list on page 75 for some smart ways to stock up a self-serve snack pantry so kids always have a healthy option when that attack hits!

MENU

Wa-s'up? Tuna Salad
  Pinwheels
Cold Ginger, Soy, and Honey
  Sesame Noodles
Pseudo Sushi
PB&J Extreme
Lunch Box Fun-due
Danish Lunch Box Smorrebrod
Meatball and Orzo Soup
Chicken Taco Soup
My Mom's Baked Apples
Chili-Cheese Dogs in Beach
  Blankets
Chicks in a Sleeping Bag and
  Crispy Salad with Mandarin
  Oranges

Apple-Jack Quesadillas
Lady Bug Pizzas
Individual Chicken Quesadillas
  Suiza

BENTO BOX LUNCH

A bento box is a groovy set of Japanese dishes that fit inside one compact box with separate compartments for each course of a meal. This really fun and funky lunch is made up of three different recipes, but each is so easy, you can make it in minutes! Bring along some chopsticks to eat your bento box lunch and you really will be too cool for school!

Wa-s'up? Tuna Salad Pinwheels

INGREDIENTS

- ¼ teaspoon **wasabi paste** (a blob the size of a pea)
- 2 tablespoons **tamari** or soy sauce (eyeball it)
- 1 tablespoon **canola** or vegetable oil
- 2 **scallions**, white and green parts, chopped
- 1 (6-ounce) can **water-packed tuna**, drained and flaked with a fork
- 1 (10- to 12-inch) **spinach flour tortilla**
- 1 cup fresh **baby spinach**, chopped

> **THE ITTY BITTIES CAN:**
> - drain and flake tuna
> - roll up pinwheels

INSTRUCTIONS

In a small bowl, mix the wasabi with the tamari and the oil. Add the scallions and tuna, and mash with a fork to combine.

Heat a large skillet over high heat and blister the tortilla for about 30 seconds on each side to soften and toast. Let the tortilla cool for about 1 minute.

Spread the tortilla with an even layer of the tuna salad and sprinkle evenly with the spinach. Fold 2 sides of the tortilla in at the edges, then roll up the tortilla tightly. Cut into 2-inch-thick slices to make the pinwheels.

SERVES 1

Cold Ginger, Soy, and Honey Sesame Noodles

If you like, add some steamed veggies, like broccoli florets.

- 1 tablespoon **smooth peanut butter**
- 1 tablespoon **honey**
- 2 tablespoons **tamari** or soy sauce (eyeball it)
- 1 teaspoon **sesame oil** (eyeball it)
- 1 teaspoon **ground ginger** or 1-inch piece of fresh ginger, peeled and grated
- ¼ pound **whole-wheat spaghetti**, cooked and rinsed under cold water
- 1 tablespoon **toasted sesame seeds** (optional)

> ### THE ITTY BITTIES CAN:
>
> - measure ingredients
> - whisk sauce
> - toss spaghetti

INSTRUCTIONS

In a medium-size microwaveable bowl, heat the peanut butter in the microwave oven on high until melted, 15 to 20 seconds. (You can also heat the peanut butter in a saucepan over low heat on the stovetop.) Whisk the honey and tamari into the peanut butter, then whisk in the sesame oil and the ginger. Toss the spaghetti with the sauce. If you want to get really groovy with the noodles, sprinkle them with sesame seeds. If you want to bump up the crunch factor, add some shredded carrots, scallions, bean sprouts, or other veggies.

SERVES 1

Pseudo Sushi

- 4 large **marshmallows** or 1 cup mini marshmallows
- 1 tablespoon **butter**
- ½ cup **puffed rice cereal**
- 2 cherry or strawberry **licorice twists**, such as Twizzlers or Red Vines
- 2 **fruit roll-ups**, any flavor

THE ITTY BITTIES CAN:

- stir cereal and marshmallow mixture
- cut licorice
- roll up sushi

INSTRUCTIONS

In a small saucepan, melt the marshmallows with the butter over low heat, stirring constantly. Add the rice cereal and stir to coat; let cool slightly. Cut the licorice sticks to the length of the fruit roll-up. Unroll the fruit roll-up and peel off the plastic film. Place half of the rice cereal mixture along one long edge of each roll-up. Place the twist in the center of the rice cereal mixture and roll up the candy sushi. Dip a knife in water to keep it from sticking and cut into 2-inch pieces.

SERVES 1

MORE IDEAS

Come up with your own "sushi" combos or use some of ours, below. Invest in a set of mini cookie cutters to make anything from cheese to veggies and fruits look cute and extra yum-o!

- Roast beef, Swiss cheese, mustard, romaine, cucumber spears
- Negi-Mock-y: roast beef, soy mayo, cooked scallions
- Turkey, wasabi mayo, green bean, red pepper strip
- Ham, honey mustard, grated mozzarella, pickle spear
- All veg: blanched chard leaf, cooked asparagus, carrot, pepper, eggplant strips, sun-dried tomatoes
- Thanksgiving Roll: turkey, mashed potatoes, cranberry sauce, peas

Wrap, roll, and slice.

WHOLE GRAINS—HALFWAY

Have some whole-grain skeptics in your house? Try going half and half rather than making the switch entirely. For your next PB&J or grilled cheese sandwich, use one slice of whole-grain bread and one slice of regular white bread. Cut the sandwich in quarters diagonally and flip two of the triangles for a cool checkerboard sammie.

You can mix it up with pasta, too. Just add the whole-wheat pasta to your boiling water first and, after it has cooked for about 2 minutes, add the regular pasta and cook until both are al dente. Sauce and serve. (Check your pasta packages for cooking times, as they can vary, and adjust accordingly.)

buffalo ranch club sandwich

KID 2 KID

SUBMITTED BY CANDIDA S. AND HER DAUGHTER ADRIANNA (AGE THIRTEEN) FROM CONNEAUT LAKE, PENNSYLVANIA

Adrianna is often required to supervise her siblings during the day, which includes making their lunch. She decided one day to make a kid-friendly version of Rachael's buffalo ranch chicken club sandwich, which requires no stovetop cooking whatsoever.

1 to 2 tablespoons prepared ranch dressing • A couple shakes of hot sauce • 2 slices honey ham • 2 slices smoked turkey • 1 slice tomato • 2 slices whole-grain bread

In a small bowl, stir together the ranch dressing and hot sauce.

Put the ham on a plate with the turkey and the slice of tomato and microwave for 30 seconds on high. Flip the stack and microwave for another 15 seconds. Slide the stack onto a piece of bread and spoon the ranch mixture over the top. Add the second slice of bread, cut in half, and enjoy.

MAKES 1 SANDWICH

PB&J Extreme

Heads-up: many schools don't allow PB&J in the lunch rooms anymore because some kids are super allergic to peanuts. So check first before packing it in the lunch box. If you can't have it at school, serve it at home for a weekend lunch or even breakfast!

INGREDIENTS

- 2 tablespoons **chunky peanut butter**
- 2 slices **whole-wheat bread**, toasted
- ½ **banana**, thinly sliced
  Drizzle of **honey**
  Sprinkle of **ground cinnamon**
- 2 slices crispy cooked **turkey bacon**, crumbled

THE ITTY BITTIES CAN:
- drizzle honey
- sprinkle cinnamon
- crumble bacon

INSTRUCTIONS

Spread the peanut butter on 1 slice of the toast. Arrange the banana slices on top of the peanut butter, drizzle with honey, then sprinkle with cinnamon. Top with bacon crumbles and the second slice of toast. Cut corner to corner to make 4 triangles.

SERVES 1

Lunch Box Fun-due

INGREDIENTS

- ½ cup **turkey breast**, cut into bite-size pieces
- ½ cup **boiled ham**, cut into bite-size pieces
- ½ cup **Cheddar**, Provolone, American, or Monterey Jack cheese, cut into bite-size cubes
- 2 medium **carrots**, peeled and cut into sticks
- 2 **celery ribs**, cut into sticks
- 3 tablespoons **jarred salsa**
- 3 tablespoons **ranch dressing**, homemade (see page 196) or a good-quality all-natural brand
- 1 slice **angel food cake**, cut into bite-size pieces
- ½ pint **strawberries**, hulled

> **THE ITTY BITTIES CAN:**
> - cut up cheeses
> - peel vegetables
> - cut cake
> - hull strawberries

INSTRUCTIONS

Pack all the different savory components in separate resealable plastic bags or containers. Mix the salsa and ranch dressing in a small plastic container for savory dipping.

Place the cake cubes in another plastic food-storage bag or container. Puree the strawberries with a splash of water or juice in a blender and pour into a small plastic container for sweet dipping.

Pack everything into a lunch box. Lunchtime today will be interactive and dip-a-licious!

SERVES 1

> **DID LETTERMAN PACK MY LUNCH?**
>
> Buy a kids' joke book and jot a joke down, personalizing it with your kid's name or a pet's name. Joke of the Day goes over a lot bigger than those embarrassing inspirational notes some parents sneak into lunch boxes.

Danish Lunch Box Smorrebrod

In Denmark little open-faced sandwiches (that means they have no tops on them) are lunchtime and snack-time favorites of kids and grown-ups alike. Try a mix-and-match of these three sammies and your box will rock—Danish style.

INGREDIENTS

- 1 tablespoon **butter**, softened
- ¼ teaspoon **sweet paprika**
- 3 slices whole-grain, pumpernickel, or rye **bread**
- 1 slice **ham** or **smoky salami**
- 1 teaspoon raspberry or red currant **fruit spread**
- 1 slice **herb-roasted turkey breast**
- 1 thin slice of Fontina or Swiss **cheese**
- 2 tablespoons soft **cream cheese** or spreadable goat cheese
  A sprinkle of chopped **dill**, fresh or dried
- 1 **radish**, sliced
- 4 **cucumber slices**

SAMMIE #1

Mix ½ tablespoon of the butter with the paprika. Spread 1 slice of the bread with the butter, then top with the ham or smoky salami. Cut into 4 squares.

SAMMIE #2

Mix the remaining ½ tablespoon butter with the raspberry or red currant fruit spread. Spread 1 slice of the bread with the butter and top with the turkey and Fontina or Swiss cheese. Cut into 4 squares.

Spread the cream cheese or goat cheese on the remaining slice of bread and top with the dill, radish, and cucumber. Cut into 4 squares.

Pack up some celery sticks and baby carrots to munch along with your smorrebrod lunch!

Meatball and Orzo *S*oup

This is a great way to fill up a thermos! Orzo's shape is fun, and so is rolling the little meatballs!

INGREDIENTS

- 1 tablespoon EVOO (extra-virgin olive oil), once around the pan
- ½ small onion, finely chopped
- 1 carrot, peeled and grated or finely chopped
- 4 cups (1 quart) chicken stock
- ½ pound ground chicken or turkey breast
- 3 tablespoons Parmigiano-Reggiano cheese
- 3 tablespoons bread crumbs
- 1 egg
- 1 garlic clove, grated
- 2 tablespoons chopped fresh flat-leaf parsley
  Salt and freshly ground black pepper
- ½ cup orzo

> **THE ITTY BITTIE*S* CAN:**
> - peel and grate carrot
> - roll meatballs

INSTRUCTIONS

Heat the EVOO in a medium pot over medium heat. Sauté the onions and carrots for 5 minutes, then add the stock and bring to a boil. In a medium bowl, mix the meat with the cheese, bread crumbs, egg, garlic, parsley, salt, and pepper. If the mixture is too moist, add a few more bread crumbs.

When the broth comes to a boil, roll the meat mixture into 1-inch balls and drop them into the broth. Stir in the orzo and cook for 5 minutes. The pasta will not be done but it will continue to cook as the soup sits. Ladle the soup into thermoses. (If you are making the soup to serve at home, continue cooking until the orzo is tender, another 2 or 3 minutes.)

MAKES 2 BIG THERMOSFULS, ABOUT 6 CUPS

A THERMOS THAT ROCKS!
Chicken Taco Soup

INGREDIENTS

½	cup	**jarred mild green salsa** (salsa verde)
1	cup	shredded or chopped **cooked chicken**
		Salt and **freshly ground black pepper**
1½	cups	**chicken stock**
½	cup	**whole-grain tortilla chips**, crushed
¼	cup	shredded **sharp Cheddar cheese**

THE ITTY
BITTIES CAN:

- shred chicken
- crush tortilla chips
- shred cheese

INSTRUCTIONS

In a medium sauce pot combine the salsa and chicken. Season with salt and pepper and stir in the chicken stock. Heat the soup over medium heat and transfer to a thermos. Pack the chips and cheese in small resealable plastic bags.

At lunchtime, kids can pile up some crushed chips and cheese and pour soup over the top to eat. Yum-o!

SERVES 2

special ham and cheese sandwich

SUBMITTED BY EVETTE P. AND DAUGHTER CHARNELLE
(AGE SIXTEEN) OF CHICAGO, ILLINOIS

Charnelle came up with this nifty sammie for her dad one afternoon.

½ tablespoon softened butter • 2 slices crusty bread, toasted • 3 slices deli ham
• 2 tablespoons pickle juice • 2 slices Cheddar cheese • 2 tablespoons mustard
(optional)

Spread the butter on the toasted bread.

Heat a small skillet over medium heat. Add the ham and brown on one side. Drizzle with
1 tablespoon of the pickle juice and turn to brown the second side. When the ham is almost
done, add the Cheddar cheese and let it melt on top of the ham. Transfer the ham and
cheese to one of the bread slices. Mix the mustard, if using, with the remaining pickle juice
and drizzle it over the cheese. Place the other slice of bread on top and there you have it.

MAKES 1 SANDWICH

FRUITY WATER

Bottled water that has been enhanced with fruit juice and extra nutrients is popular with kids and their parents, too, and for good reason: it contains a lot less sugar than soda or sports drinks and provides a bit of extra nutrition. The downside? Enhanced water tends to be pricey and then there's the issue of all those plastic bottles to recycle! Make your own at home on the cheap and you can refill your own sport bottles to your heart's content—and stash the money you save in a pizza-and-movie fund!

Combine the flavoring blend ingredients of your choice in a glass mixing cup with a spout. Pour the mixture into an ice-cube tray and freeze until completely solid, then transfer the cubes to heavy-duty freezer bags.

Be sure to use 100-percent unsweetened juice and juice concentrates (look in the natural foods aisle or in your local health food store; Lakewood and Knudsen make good ones) for the best flavor. Create your own signature blends.

bpb quesadillas

SUBMITTED BY TAVYN W. (AGE NINE)
FROM NORTH LITTLE ROCK, ARKANSAS

2 whole-wheat flour tortillas • 2 tablespoons peanut butter, smooth or chunky • 1 banana, cut in ¼-inch-thick slices

Spread both tortillas with the peanut butter. Arrange the banana slices on one of the tortillas and top with the second tortilla. Heat in a nonstick skillet until lightly browned on both sides and gooey. Cut in wedges and serve.

SERVES 1 OR 2

chicken and asparagus wrap

SUBMITTED BY FAITH B. AND HER DAUGHTER SAMANTHA
(AGE ELEVEN) FROM BARRIE, ONTARIO, CANADA

1 bunch of asparagus, ends trimmed • 6 whole-wheat flour tortillas • 1 cup hummus, any flavor • 2 cups cooked chicken, shredded or cut in strips • 6 slices Swiss cheese

Steam the asparagus until tender; cool slightly. Spread each tortilla with a few tablespoons of hummus and top with a few asparagus spears. Add a handful of chicken to each and cover that with a slice of Swiss cheese. Roll the wrap like a fajita and enjoy!

SERVES 3 TO 4

My Mom's Baked Apples

This is a fave of mine from back in the day!
Eat more apples!

INGREDIENTS

- 4 **McIntosh apples**, all about the same size (see Note)
- ⅔ cup **Grape-Nuts cereal**
- ½ teaspoon **ground cinnamon**
- ¼ teaspoon **freshly grated nutmeg**
- 2 tablespoons **brown sugar**, packed
- 2 tablespoons **cold butter**, diced
- ⅓ cup chopped **walnuts**, a couple of handfuls
- 2 tablespoons **currants**

> **THE ITTY BITTIES CAN:**
> - measure ingredients
> - chop walnuts
> - mix stuffing
> - stuff apples

INSTRUCTIONS

Preheat the oven to 350°F.

Cut an X at the stem end of each apple, then use a spoon to scoop halfway into each apple, making a cavity and removing the core. Trim the bottoms if necessary to make sure the apples stand upright. Place the apples in a small baking dish. Mix the cereal with the cinnamon, nutmeg, brown sugar, butter, nuts, and currants. Stuff the cereal mixture into the apples and bake for 30 to 35 minutes, or until the apples are tender and the filling is brown and bubbly. Serve hot as is or top with ice cream for an upside-down apple sundae. Yum-o!

SERVES 4

NOTE: You can make this recipe with tart and tangy Granny Smith apples, too, but you will need to bake them for 45 to 50 minutes because they are much firmer apples.

Chili-Cheese Dogs in Beach Blankets

What's cooler than a corn dog? A chili dog with cheese in a blanket! Check out this walk-around-and-eat-it summer fun dog with the works!

I'm sending a shout-out to my friend Rob Walls, who gave me the big idea of Frankenstuffers, which are sauerkraut and mustard–wrapped dogs. These Chili-Cheese Dogs in Beach Blankets would not be possible without your big, bright ideas, fella!

INGREDIENTS

- 1 tablespoon vegetable oil or EVOO (extra-virgin olive oil)
- ¾ pound ground beef, ground turkey, or tempeh chopped into fine crumbles
- 1 tablespoon chili powder, a palmful
- 1 teaspoon granulated garlic
- 2 teaspoons dehydrated onion
  Salt and freshly ground black pepper
- 2 tablespoons tomato paste
- 1 (13.8-ounce) tube refrigerator pizza dough
- 1½ cups shredded Cheddar cheese
- 8 turkey or tofu dogs

> **THE ITTY BITTIES CAN:**
> - measure ingredients
> - shred cheese
> - roll dogs in blankets

INSTRUCTIONS

Preheat the oven to 400°F.

Heat the oil in a small pot over medium-high heat. Add the meat to the pot and brown it up, 6 to 7 minutes. Season the meat with the chili powder, granulated garlic, dehydrated onion, and a little salt and pepper. Add the tomato paste to the

pot and stir it around for a minute, then add ¼ cup water to help loosen the tomato paste and get it incorporated. Turn the heat down to low and simmer for 5 minutes, then turn off the heat.

Roll out the pizza dough into a big rectangle. Cut the dough in half lengthwise with a small knife. Cut the dough into 4 equal pieces across so that you end up with 8 small rectangular pieces of dough. Across the center of each rectangle place a couple of spoonfuls of chili sauce and sprinkle a small handful of cheese on top. Set the dog on the dough and wrap and roll the pizza dough around the dog as you would for pigs in a blanket, sealing in the chili and cheese. The nubs of each end of the dog should be peeking out. Arrange on a baking sheet and bake for 18 minutes, or until golden. Yum-o!

SERVES 8

Chicks in a Sleeping Bag and Crispy Salad with Mandarin Oranges

Forget pigs in a blanket; check out these chickies! The apricot-preserve sauce does double duty in this recipe as a dip for the chicks and a tangy salad dressing.

INGREDIENTS

- ½ cup **apricot all-fruit spread**
- ¼ cup **honey** (eyeball it)
- 2 tablespoons **tamari** or soy sauce
- 1 tablespoon **cider vinegar**, rice wine vinegar, or white wine vinegar
- 3 tablespoons **canola or vegetable oil**
- 3 tablespoons spicy brown, Dijon, or yellow **mustard**, whichever you prefer
- ½ sheet **frozen puff pastry dough**, such as Pepperidge Farm, thawed
- 4 precooked **chicken sausages**, any flavor
- 2 tablespoons **sesame seeds** or poppy seeds (optional)
- ½ head of **iceberg lettuce**, chopped
- 1 (6-ounce) can **mandarin orange segments**, drained
- ¼ **seedless cucumber**, sliced
  Salt and **freshly ground black pepper**

> **THE ITTY BITTIES CAN:**
>
> - measure ingredients
> - assemble chicks in sleeping bags
> - toss salad

Preheat the oven to 425°F.

In a medium mixing bowl, stir together the apricot preserves and honey. Pour one third of the apricot mixture into the bottom of a salad bowl and whisk in the tamari and vinegar. Add the oil in a slow stream, whisking, to make your salad dressing. Stir the mustard into the remaining apricot-honey mixture for the chicks in blankets and dipping sauce.

Cut the pastry into 4 rectangles. Spread a little apricot-honey mustard on each rectangle, then roll up the sausages in the blankets and pinch at the seams to keep the chicks in their "sleeping bags." Brush the tops of the sleeping bags with a dab of the mustard for gloss and color; sprinkle with sesame seeds, if using; and arrange on a nonstick baking sheet. Bake according to the puff pastry package directions, or until golden brown all over, about 12 to15 minutes.

While the chicks are in the oven, add the lettuce, mandarin oranges, and cucumbers to the salad bowl. Toss with the dressing and season with salt and pepper.

Arrange the chicks on plates. Pile up the salad alongside, unless you hate it when your food touches, in which case use a separate salad bowl. Pass the remaining sauce for topping or dipping. De-lish!

SERVES 4

TIDBIT
Precooked chicken sausages come in lots of cool flavors such as apple, Thai-seasoned, spinach, or roasted garlic. They are low in fat and they cook in just a few minutes. Look for them in the packaged meat case near the hot dogs.

lunch boxes that rock and snack-attackers

Apple-Jack Quesadillas

INGREDIENTS

- 4 teaspoons EVOO (extra-virgin olive oil)
- 4 tablespoons pepper jelly
- 4 (10- to 12-inch) whole-wheat flour tortillas
- 2 cups shredded Monterey Jack or pepper Jack cheese, 4 generous handfuls
- 1 McIntosh apple, quartered, cored, and thinly sliced

THE ITTY BITTIES CAN:

- shred cheese
- slice apples
- assemble quesadillas

INSTRUCTIONS

Preheat the oven to 150°F.

Preheat a teaspoon of the EVOO in a nonstick skillet over medium heat. Spread 1 tablespoon of pepper jelly on a tortilla and place it in the pan, jelly side up. Cover half the tortilla with about ½ cup cheese and one fourth of the apple slices. Fold the naked half of the tortilla over and cook for a couple of minutes on each side until the quesadilla is brown and crispy and the cheese is melted. Keep in the oven while you make 3 additional quesadillas.

Cut each quesadilla in 4 wedges and serve.

SERVES 4

Lady Bug Pizzas

Who knew bugs could be so tasty?

INGREDIENTS

- 4 tablespoons **pesto**, store-bought or homemade
- 2 sandwich-size **whole-wheat English muffins**, split
- 1 cup shredded **Provolone** or mozzarella cheese
- 4 slices of ripe **tomato**
- ¼ cup pitted **black olives**, chopped

THE ITTY BITTIES CAN:

- shred cheese
- chop olives
- assemble pizzas

INSTRUCTIONS

Preheat the oven or toaster oven to 400°F.

Spread 1 tablespoon of the pesto on each muffin half. Top each "pizza" with ¼ cup cheese. Top the cheese with a slice of tomato and scatter the olives over the tomato to look like the dots on lady bug backs. Bake for 7 to 8 minutes or until very crisp and the cheese has melted. Serve warm.

SERVES 4

Individual Chicken Quesadillas Suiza

Leftover chicken or turkey goes Tex-Mex in this easy lunch or supper that is totally yum-o!

INGREDIENTS

- 1 cup shredded or chopped white-meat chicken or turkey
- ¼ cup mild or medium green chile or tomatillo salsa (salsa verde)
- 2 teaspoons EVOO (extra-virgin olive oil)
- 2 (8-inch) whole-wheat or spinach flour tortillas
- 1 cup shredded Monterey Jack cheese or queso fresco
- 1 scallion, white and green parts, chopped
  A small handful of chopped Spanish green olives with pimiento
- 1 teaspoon chopped fresh cilantro or flat-leaf parsley

> **THE ITTY BITTIES CAN:**
> - shred chicken
> - shred cheese
> - chop scallion, olives, and herbs

INSTRUCTIONS

Preheat the broiler.

Toss the chicken or turkey with the salsa to combine.

Heat 1 teaspoon of the EVOO in an ovenproof skillet over medium to medium-high heat. Add a tortilla, crisp it up on both sides, about 1 minute total, and remove. Add another teaspoon of oil and the second tortilla. Cook until the first side is crisp, turn it, top it with the chicken or turkey, and place the other tortilla on top. Sprinkle the quesadilla with the cheese, scallions, and olives and pop the pan under the broiler for 1 to 2 minutes to melt and bubble the cheese. Slide the quesadilla out of the pan and cut in quarters. Sprinkle with the cilantro or parsley and serve.

SERVES 4

SNACK PANTRY

Designate one kitchen shelf and one shelf or drawer in the fridge, if there's room, just for healthy snacks, things kids can grab whenever they need a little something between meals. Pack up kid-size portions in small zip-closure bags or plastic containers so they're ready to tuck in lunch boxes or backpacks. Here are some ideas to get you started.

PANTRY

Pita chips

Rice cakes

Whole-grain pretzels

Whole-grain tortilla chips

Dried fruit (apples, pears, apricots, pineapple, and more)

Whole almonds

Popcorn (top with Parm and dried Italian seasoning)

Peanut butter

FRIDGE

Cinnamon-flavored applesauce

Hummus

Guacamole

Salsa

Baba ghanoush (roasted eggplant dip)

Canned white beans pureed with garlic and herbs

Apple slices with peanut butter

Baby carrots with Bunny Spread (see page 27)

Cold chicken fingers (page 184 or 186)

Yogurt with granola topping or fruit

Cheese sticks (think Cheddar, Muenster, and pepper Jack, not just mozzarella)

Olives

Veggie sticks, such as carrot, bell pepper, zucchini, snap peas

Boiled edamame in the pod

And, of course, lots of healthy drinks preloaded into sport bottles or sippy cups.

It's All in the Numbers

I've always said you don't need to spend more than thirty minutes in the kitchen to throw down a great meal that is healthier and tastier than anything you could order in, and I still live (and cook) by that philosophy. Sometimes, though, investing an extra ten or fifteen minutes one night can mean a huge savings of time down the line, as with my rollover suppers, which allow you to cook once and eat twice (or even three or four times!) with minimal extra work. Why not poach up a couple of extra chicken breasts or make a jumbo batch of turkey Bolognese sauce if it means they can do double duty a day or two later? Believe me, you'll thank me when you can get a steaming bowl of turkey chili on the table fifteen minutes after you roll in the door. Also included in this section are multiple-choice suppers, such as chicken for picky, not-so-picky, and adventurous eaters all in the same meal or eggplant steaks, three ways. So while the kids are doing *their* homework, do some new math of your own, with these three-way recipes, two-for-ones, and other great meal ideas. It's all in the numbers!

MENU

Rollover Supper: Jerk Chicken with Roasted Vegetables and Pineapple; Sweet and Spicy Sesame Noodles with Shredded Chicken; and Jerk Chicken Quesadillas with Slaw Salad

5-10-15 in 30-Minute Meal Dinner: Caprese Mezzaluna; Chicken and Broccolini with Asiago Sauce; and Italian Sponge Cakes in 5

Rollover Supper: Turkey Stuffin' Meatloaf with Scallion Mashed Potatoes and Green Beans; and Enchi-lasagna

Rollover Supper: Turkey Bolognese Pasta; Turkey Tomato Soup; and Turkey Vegetable Chili

Three Quick Skillet Sauces for Chicken: Skillet Barbecue Gravy; Apple Cider Gravy; and Orange-Maple Reduction

Chicken Noodle Soup, Three Ways: Quick Traditional Chicken Noodle Soup; Chicken

Noodle Soup Latin Style; Chicken Noodle Soup Italian Style

Rollover Supper: My Mom's Top-Secret Chicken Curry with Rice; Chicken Soup with Broken Spaghetti

Tuna Two Times: Creamy Tuna with Tarragon and Egg Noodles; Spicy Tomato and Tuna Spaghetti

Grilled Eggplant—Three Ways: Chicken-Eggplant Steak Roll-up Salad; Eggplant Steak Lasagna Stacks; and Meat and Mushroom Eggplant Roll-ups with Tomato Gravy

NIGHT 1: Jerk Chicken with Roasted Vegetables and Pineapple

Add a DVD of Johnny Depp as a pirate and you've got a night in the Caribbean, plus a head start on two more dinners. Arrrh!

INGREDIENTS

- 3 **red onions**, 1 coarsely chopped and 2 sliced
- 4 **garlic cloves**, coarsely chopped
- 4 **scallions**, green and white parts, coarsely chopped
  Juice of 2 limes
- 2 **jalapeño peppers**, halved and seeded
- 3 tablespoons **red wine vinegar**
- ½ cup **orange juice**
- 1 tablespoon **sweet paprika**, a palmful
- 1 tablespoon **ground cumin,** a palmful
- 2 teaspoons **ground allspice**, about ⅔ palmful
- ½ teaspoon **ground cinnamon**, eyeball it in your palm
- 5 to 6 **fresh thyme** sprigs
- ½ cup **EVOO** (extra-virgin olive oil), plus 2 to 3 tablespoons for drizzling
- 8 **chicken drumsticks**
- 8 **bone-in, skin-on chicken breasts**
  Salt and **freshly ground black pepper**
- 1 **pineapple**, peeled, cored, and chopped into small bite-size pieces
- 1 **yellow bell pepper**, seeded and chopped or sliced
- 2 **red bell peppers**, seeded and chopped or sliced
- 1 **green bell pepper**, seeded and chopped or sliced

> ### THE ITTY BITTIES CAN:
> - pulse food processor
> - measure spices
> - cut pineapple

(recipe continues)

Preheat the oven to 400°F.

Place the chopped red onion in a food processor with the garlic, scallions, lime juice, jalapeño peppers, red wine vinegar, orange juice, paprika, cumin, allspice, cinnamon, and thyme. Pulse to combine. With the processor running, stream in the ½ cup EVOO to form a thick paste.

Season the chicken pieces generously with salt and pepper, then rub all over with the spice paste. Arrange the chicken in a roasting pan and roast uncovered for 45 minutes.

Pile the pineapple, bell peppers, and sliced red onions on a rimmed baking sheet, coat them in 2 to 3 tablespoons EVOO, and season with salt and pepper. Add the baking sheet to the oven after the chicken has been in for 15 minutes and roast the fruit and vegetables along with the chicken for about 30 minutes.

Serve up half the chicken (one drummer and one piece of breast per person) and half of the roasted pineapple, peppers, and onions for dinner.

Cool the leftovers before you wrap and refrigerate them.

SERVES 4

NIGHT 2: Sweet and Spicy Sesame Noodles with Shredded Chicken

INGREDIENTS

Salt
1 pound **spaghetti**, whole wheat or plain
½ cup **chicken stock**
    1-inch piece of **fresh ginger**, peeled and grated,
    or 1 teaspoon ground ginger
1 **garlic clove**, grated
3 tablespoons **peanut butter**
¼ cup **tamari** or soy sauce

Hot sauce, a couple of dashes

2   tablespoons **canola oil**

2   tablespoons **honey**

Half of the remaining **jerk chicken**, skin removed and meat shredded, about 2 cups

Half of the remaining **roasted pineapple, peppers, and onions**

1   (16-ounce) bag of **slaw mix** (shredded cabbage and carrots)

4   **scallions**, green and white parts, thinly sliced on an angle

3   tablespoons **toasted sesame seeds**

INSTRUCTIONS

Place a large pot of water over high heat and bring to a boil. Once the water is boiling, add a generous amount of salt and the pasta and cook al dente.

While the pasta is cooking, heat the chicken stock in a small saucepan. Once warm, add the ginger, garlic, peanut butter, tamari, hot sauce, canola oil, and honey and whisk to combine.

In a large bowl combine the shredded chicken; the roasted pineapple, peppers, and onions; and 2 cups of the shredded cabbage mix. (Reserve the rest of the slaw mix for the next rollover supper.)

Drain the pasta and add to the bowl with the chicken. Pour the sauce over the noodles and toss to combine. Garnish with the scallions and sesame seeds.

SERVES 4

NIGHT 3: Jerk Chicken Quesadillas with Slaw Salad

INGREDIENTS

Juice of 1 lime

2 tablespoons rice wine vinegar or white wine vinegar

2 tablespoons tamari or soy sauce

Hot sauce, a dash or two

3 tablespoons honey

3 tablespoons canola oil

Salt and freshly ground black pepper

½ seedless cucumber, cut into matchsticks

3 scallions, thinly sliced

Remaining slaw mix from Night 2 (about ¾ pound)

4 large whole-wheat flour tortillas

Remaining pineapple and vegetable mixture

Remaining jerk chicken, skin removed and meat shredded

2 cups shredded Monterey Jack, pepper Jack, or smoked Cheddar

INSTRUCTIONS

In a large bowl, mix together the lime juice, vinegar, tamari, hot sauce, and honey. Whisk in the canola oil in a slow stream and season with salt and pepper. Add the cucumber, scallions, and the slaw mix and toss to combine well.

Place a large skillet over medium heat. Add 1 tortilla to the pan and cook for about 1 minute on each side, or until it is starting to blister. Pile a quarter of the pineapple and vegetable mixture, a quarter of the shredded chicken, and a quarter of the cheese on one half of the tortilla and fold the other half over the filling to create a half moon. Cook the quesadilla until the cheese is melted, flipping it halfway through. Keep the quesadilla warm in a low (200°F) oven while you make the remaining quesadillas. Cut into wedges and serve with the slaw salad.

SERVES 4

joe's fish tacos

SUBMITTED BY CECILIA M.

Cecilia likes to make this healthy dish with her fourteen-month-old son, Joe, who already loves to eat all kinds of food!

2 teaspoons EVOO (extra-virgin olive oil) • 1 pound whitefish fillets, such as cod, halibut, or sole • 1 cup mild or medium salsa • 4 flour tortillas

TOPPINGS

Shredded Monterey Jack • Sliced avocado • Sliced tomato • Sliced red onion

Heat the EVOO in a large sauté pan over medium-high heat. Add the fish fillets and cook until the flesh is firm and opaque. Add the salsa to the pan and stir, breaking up the fish into large chunks.

Spoon the fish filling into the tortillas and serve with a platter of toppings.

SERVES 4

hannah's awesome salsa

SUBMITTED BY KAREN G. AND HER DAUGHTER HANNAH (AGE ELEVEN) FROM LONGMEADOW, MASSACHUSETTS

Hannah chops up all the ingredients and mixes them together for a delicious non-runny salsa. She makes it for her family at least four nights a week. Some nights she adds an avocado for guacamole.

2 plum tomatoes, seeded and chopped • 1 red bell pepper, seeded and finely chopped • 1 yellow bell pepper, seeded and finely chopped • 1 seedless cucumber, finely chopped • 1 red onion, finely chopped • ½ cup chopped fresh cilantro • Salt and freshly ground black pepper

In a medium bowl, stir together the tomatoes, bell peppers, cucumber, red onion, cilantro, salt, and black pepper. Let the salsa sit for a few hours, if you can resist, to let the flavors blend together.

MAKES 2 CUPS

Italian Sponge Cakes in 5, Caprese Mezzaluna in 10, and Chicken and Broccolini with Asiago Sauce in 15

What can you make in five minutes? In ten? In thirty minutes you can make all three of these dishes for a full, three-course meal. Pretty neat, huh?

CAPRESE MEZZALUNA

INGREDIENTS

- ⅓ to ½ cup EVOO (extra-virgin olive oil)
- 2 garlic cloves, crushed
- 4 (10- to 12-inch) flour tortillas
- 1 8-ounce ball fresh mozzarella, thinly sliced
- 12 fresh basil leaves, shredded
- 2 ripe tomatoes, thinly sliced
  Salt and freshly ground black pepper

THE ITTY
BITTIES CAN:

- assemble mezzalunas

INSTRUCTIONS

To make the appetizers, heat the oil with the garlic in a small pot until the oil bubbles. Turn the heat to very low and simmer for a minute. Brush a skillet with some of the garlic oil (save the rest for cooking the chicken) and heat over medium-high heat. Add a tortilla to the hot skillet and blister it for 30 seconds, then flip it.

Cover half of the surface with a layer of mozzarella, basil, and tomato, season with salt and pepper, and fold the other half over. Cook the "Italian quesadilla" for 30 seconds on each side, then transfer to a plate. Make 3 more quesadillas. Cut into quarters and serve.

SERVES 4

CHICKEN AND BROCCOLINI WITH ASIAGO SAUCE

INGREDIENTS

- 4 boneless, skinless chicken breasts
  Salt and freshly ground black pepper
- 1 bundle of broccolini, 1 inch of stems removed
- 2 tablespoons butter
- 1 rounded tablespoon all-purpose flour
- 1½ cups milk
- 1 cup grated Asiago cheese
  Freshly grated nutmeg

THE ITTY
BITTIES CAN:

- trim broccolini
- grate cheese

INSTRUCTIONS

Heat a couple tablespoons of the garlic oil in a skillet over medium-high heat. Season the chicken with salt and pepper and cook for 6 minutes on each side, turning once, until it is golden and the juices run clear. While the chicken cooks, heat 1 inch of water over high heat in a small, deep skillet. When it boils, add salt and the broccolini to the water and cook for 3 to 4 minutes; drain and reserve. Meanwhile, heat the butter over medium heat in a small sauce pot. Stir the flour into the melted butter, cook for 1 minute, then whisk in the milk and cook until thickened, 2 to 3 minutes. Stir in the cheese and season with the nutmeg, salt, and pepper. Serve the chicken topped with the broccolini and pour the sauce over the top. In less than 15 minutes you have a low-maintenance chicken divan!

SERVES 4

ITALIAN SPONGE CAKES IN 5

INGREDIENTS

- ⅓ cup **honey** (eyeball it)
- 4 individual **sponge cake shells**
- 1 pint **vanilla ice cream**
- 8 **strawberries**, hulled and sliced

> ### THE ITTY BITTIES CAN:
> - douse and fill cakes
> - slice berries

INSTRUCTIONS

Heat the honey and a splash of water in a sauce pot or in the microwave for 45 seconds to 1 minute on high. Douse the cakes with equal amounts of the sauce. Fill the shells with ice cream and top with the sliced berries.

SERVES 4

NIGHT 1: Turkey *Stuffin'* Meatloaf with *Scallion* Mashed Potatoes and Green Beans

Three popular comfort foods—meatloaf, lasagna, and enchiladas—come together to give you two tasty, well-rounded suppers: Turkey Stuffin' Meatloaf and Enchil-lasagna! Now, that's a comforting thought. It might seem like we're using a lot of butter here, but this makes a ton of gravy and it's used over two nights' meals, so don't worry too much.

INGREDIENTS

- 2 tablespoons EVOO (extra-virgin olive oil), plus some for drizzling
- 6 tablespoons butter
- 1 large onion, chopped
- 5 to 6 celery ribs from the heart with leafy tops, chopped
- 1 bay leaf
  Salt and freshly ground black pepper
- 1 (16-ounce) bag stuffing cubes, such as Pepperidge Farm
- 2 tablespoons poultry seasoning
- 6 cups (1½ quarts) chicken stock
- 3 pounds ground turkey or ground turkey breast
- 2 eggs
- 2½ pounds peeled Idaho potatoes (4 to 5 medium to large potatoes), cut into chunks
- ½ cup reduced-fat sour cream
- ½ cup milk

> THE ITTY BITTIE*S* CAN:
> - mash potatoes
> - trim beans

(recipe continues)

1 small bunch of scallions, green and white parts, chopped

¼ cup all-purpose flour

1 pound green beans, trimmed

Preheat the oven to 400°F.

In a large skillet heat the 2 tablespoons of EVOO with 2 tablespoons of the butter over medium-high heat. Add the onions, celery, and bay leaf, season with salt and pepper, and cook until tender, about 10 minutes. Add the stuffing cubes to the skillet, season with poultry seasoning, then moisten with 4 cups (1 quart) of the chicken stock. Discard the bay leaf. Place the stuffing in a bowl and cool.

Once the stuffing is cool enough to handle, add the turkey and the eggs, and season with salt and pepper. Mix the turkey with the stuffing. Form the meat mixture into 2 long loaves on a nonstick baking sheet. Drizzle the loaves with EVOO and bake for about an hour, or until the meatloaves are brown and cooked through and they register 165°F on a meat thermometer.

Once the meatloaves have cooked for about 25 minutes, start the mashed potatoes. Place the potatoes in a medium pot with water to cover. Bring to a boil and cook until tender, 12 to15 minutes. Drain the potatoes and then return to the hot pot. Add the sour cream, milk, scallions, and salt and pepper; mash and smash to your preferred consistency and adjust the seasoning.

While the potatoes are boiling, start the gravy. Melt the remaining 4 tablespoons of butter in a sauce pot. Add the flour and whisk over medium heat for 3 to 4 minutes. Whisk in the remaining 2 cups of stock and cook for 6 to 7 minutes, or until it thickens. Set aside half the gravy for tonight's meatloaf and mashed potatoes and reserve the other half for the Enchil-lasagna.

Bring 1 inch of water to a boil in a saucepan. Add salt and the green beans and cook for 3 to 4 minutes, until the beans are just tender. Drain.

Serve one meatloaf with the mashed potatoes and green beans alongside, and drizzle with the gravy.

SERVES 4, WITH SECONDS!

NIGHT 2: Enchil-lasagna

INGREDIENTS

- 3 cups **reserved gravy** from Night 1
- 1 (16 to 20-ounce) jar of **mild green chile salsa** (salsa verde)
- 8 **whole-wheat flour tortillas**
- 1 (10-ounce) box **frozen corn**, defrosted
- 1 (14-ounce) can **black beans**, rinsed and drained
- 4 to 5 **scallions**, green and white parts, chopped
- 1 **turkey meatloaf** from Night 1, thinly sliced
- 2½ cups shredded **Monterey Jack** or pepper Jack

INSTRUCTIONS

Preheat the oven to 400°F.

In a medium bowl mix the reserved gravy with the green chile salsa. Spread a thin layer of gravy salsa mixture onto the bottom of a casserole dish. Then layer in 2 tortillas, one third of the corn, one third of the black beans, one third of the scallions, one third of the sliced meatloaf, one fourth of the gravy salsa mixture, and one fourth of the cheese. Repeat this process until all of the ingredients are used. The top layer will be the last of the tortillas, a little gravy, and the remaining cheese. Bake the enchil-lasagna until the cheese is bubbling and brown, 15 to 20 minutes.

SERVES 4 TO 6

Viewers stopped me in the grocery store for weeks after this recipe aired to thank me from the bottom of their stomachs!

THE GOODS ON GREENS

Not all salad greens are created equal; in general, the darker the green, the more nutritional bang you get for your buck. If your family likes the crunch of iceberg, try switching to romaine and including some of the lighter, crisp center ribs as well as the dark outer leaves, or make your own "spring blend" by mixing in some stemmed arugula, watercress, or baby chard. For cold-night meals, heat a simple vinaigrette in the microwave for thirty seconds and pour it over sturdy greens such as escarole or spinach and slivered red onions for a wilted salad that's great with chops, broiled fish, or chicken.

Unleaded: iceberg, shredded green cabbage, Belgian endive

High-test: romaine, butter, Bibb, red leaf, radicchio, red cabbage

Premium: baby spinach, arugula, baby beet greens, dandelion greens, watercress, baby chard, mustard greens, kale, collards, chicory, escarole

ROLLOVER SUPPER

NIGHT 1: Turkey Bolognese Pasta

INGREDIENTS

- ¼ cup EVOO (extra-virgin olive oil)
- 3 pounds lean ground turkey
- 3 medium carrots, peeled and grated
- 2 onions, grated or finely chopped
- 4 garlic cloves, grated
  Salt and freshly ground black pepper
- 1 bay leaf, fresh or dry
- 2 cups regular or low-sodium chicken stock
- 2 (28-ounce) cans crushed tomatoes
- 1 pound whole-wheat spaghetti
- 1 cup grated Parmigiano-Reggiano or Romano cheese

> **THE ITTY BITTIES CAN:**
> - peel and grate carrots
> - grate onions and garlic
> - grate cheese

INSTRUCTIONS

Bring a large pot of water to a boil for the pasta.

Preheat a large Dutch oven or deep pot over medium-high heat with the EVOO, 3 to 4 times around the pan. Add the turkey and, using the back of a wooden spoon, break up the meat into small pieces. Cook for 5 to 6 minutes to start the browning process, then stir in the carrots, onions, and garlic. Season liberally with salt and pepper, add the bay leaf, and cook for 5 minutes more, then stir in the stock and the tomatoes. Bring up to a bubble, then drop the heat to low and simmer for 5 to 6 minutes more while you cook the pasta. Discard the bay leaf.

Salt the water and cook the pasta al dente, with a bite to it. Drain, then place the pasta back into the warm pot. Toss the pasta with the cheese and 2 cups of the sauce. Serve the pasta in shallow bowls with an extra ladle of sauce on top.

Cool the leftover sauce before storing in the refrigerator.

SERVES 4, PLUS MAKES 5 TO 6 CUPS LEFTOVER SAUCE

DAY 2: ROLLOVER THERMOS FILLER

Turkey Tomato Soup

INGREDIENTS

1½ cups **leftover Turkey Bolognese sauce**

1½ cups **chicken stock**

½ cup **salad croutons**, any flavor or variety

INSTRUCTIONS

Heat the sauce and stock together in a medium saucepan and serve in bowls or pack into thermoses. Serve the croutons alongside for topping.

SERVES 2

I taught a hard-working mom how to make this to launch Yum-o! on my daytime TV show. For years she and her husband had been unable to get their daughters to eat a well-balanced diet. This rollover supper has plenty of lean meat and vegetables in a rich pasta sauce and the leftovers became a simple soup and a spicy healthy chili. The mom felt so empowered that she cried—and I joined in. Serve these with a nice green salad. Good food can be good for your soul, too.

NIGHT 3: Turkey Vegetable Chili

- 2 tablespoons EVOO (extra-virgin olive oil), twice around the pan
- 2 small zucchini, grated
- 1 (10-ounce) box frozen corn
- 1 (14-ounce) can black or red beans, rinsed and drained
- 2 tablespoons chili powder
- 3 to 4 cups leftover Turkey Bolognese sauce
  Salt and freshly ground black pepper
- 1 cup shredded sharp Cheddar, Monterey Jack, pepper Jack, or smoked Cheddar cheese
  Crushed tortilla chips

INSTRUCTIONS

Preheat a large skillet over medium-high heat with the EVOO. Add the grated zucchini and cook until soft, 4 to 5 minutes. Add the frozen corn, the beans, and the chili powder. Add the Bolognese sauce and bring up to a bubble. Season with salt and pepper to taste and cook for another 5 to 6 minutes.

To serve, ladle the chili into bowls and top with cheese and crushed chips.

SERVES 4

veggie confetti

SUBMITTED BY GRETCHEN L. AND HER DAUGHTER DESTINY
(AGE NINE) FROM MIDLAND, TEXAS

We added a little zucchini to up the veggie action in Destiny's recipe!

6 plum tomatoes, seeded and chopped • Salt • 5 fresh basil leaves, finely sliced • 1 red or green bell pepper, seeded and chopped • ½ zucchini, diced • 2 garlic cloves, minced • Freshly ground black pepper • 5 tablespoons EVOO (extra-virgin olive oil) • ½ cup grated Parmigiano-Reggiano cheese • 1 whole-wheat baguette, halved lengthwise

Preheat the oven to 350°F.

Add the tomatoes to a mixing bowl, sprinkle with salt, and stir to combine. Stir in the basil, bell pepper, zucchini, garlic, black pepper, 3 tablespoons of the EVOO, and the Parm and toss to combine.

Drizzle the baguette with the remaining 2 tablespoons of EVOO and sprinkle with salt and pepper. Bake for 5 to 10 minutes, until golden brown. Spoon the veggie confetti on top and slice each half into 5 or 6 sections. Serve.

MAKES 10 TO 12 SNACK-SIZE PORTIONS

CHICKEN AGAIN? THREE SKILLET SAUCES

Here are three toppers for chicken that you can make with ingredients you have on hand, each in less than 5 minutes. Serve up your veggies of choice and some couscous, along with a five-minute super-side dish, and you have a jazzy new twist on the same ol' supper.

Each recipe will top four chicken breasts. Slice the breasts on an angle and fan them out on the plates before topping.

Skillet Barbecue Gravy

INGREDIENTS

- 2 tablespoons **butter**
- 2 tablespoons **all-purpose flour**
- 1½ cups **chicken stock**
- ¼ cup **bottled barbecue sauce**
  Salt and **freshly ground black pepper**

INSTRUCTIONS

Melt the butter in a saucepan over medium-high heat. Stir in the flour and cook, whisking, until it is light brown, 1 to 2 minutes. Whisk in the chicken stock and barbecue sauce and season with salt and pepper. Continue whisking and cook until thickened, about 3 minutes.

Apple Cider Gravy

INGREDIENTS

- 2 tablespoons butter
- 2 tablespoons all-purpose flour
- 1½ cups chicken stock
- ½ cup apple cider

Salt and freshly ground black pepper

INSTRUCTIONS

Melt the butter in a saucepan over medium-high heat. Stir in the flour and cook, whisking, until it is light brown, 1 to 2 minutes. Whisk in the chicken stock and apple cider and season with salt and pepper. Continue whisking and cook until thickened, about 3 minutes.

Orange-Maple Reduction

INGREDIENTS

- ½ cup chicken stock
- ½ cup orange juice
- ¼ cup pure maple syrup

A pinch of red pepper flakes or chili powder

Salt and freshly ground black pepper

INSTRUCTIONS

Mix the chicken stock, orange juice, maple syrup, and red pepper flakes together in a small saucepan. Bring the mixture to a bubble over high heat and cook long enough for it to reduce by half, about 5 minutes. It should be thick and syrupy. Season with salt and pepper.

CHICKEN NOODLE SOUP, THREE WAYS

Who doesn't love chicken soup? And when you make it yourself, you get more chicken and more noodles. Here are three fast soups that taste as if they were slow-cooked; and each one is so good you'll lose your noodle for it!

Quick Traditional Chicken Noodle Soup

INGREDIENTS

- 2 tablespoons EVOO (extra-virgin olive oil)
- 5 to 6 celery ribs from the heart with leafy tops, chopped
- 3 to 4 medium carrots, peeled and thinly sliced
- 1 large onion, chopped
- 1 bay leaf
  Salt and freshly ground black pepper
- 8 cups (2 quarts) chicken stock
- ½ pound extra-wide egg noodles
- 1 pound chicken tenders or chicken cutlets, cut in bite-size pieces
- ¼ cup chopped fresh dill
- 2 cups popcorn or white Cheddar popcorn, for garnish (optional)
- 1 cup oyster crackers, for garnish (optional)

INSTRUCTIONS

Heat the EVOO in a large soup pot over medium-high heat. Add the celery, carrots, onions, and bay leaf and season with salt and pepper. Cook the vegetables until tender, 8 to 10 minutes. Add the stock and bring to a boil, then stir in the egg noodles and chicken. Simmer for 5 to 6 minutes, or until the chicken is cooked through. Stir in the dill and turn off the heat. Discard the bay leaf.

Ladle the soup into bowls. Garnish with some popcorn or oyster crackers, if you like.

SERVES 6

VARIATION: Chicken Noodle Soup Latin Style

2 cups of the **chicken stock** (use 6 cups total)
Egg noodles
Dill
Garnishes

ADDITIONAL INGREDIENTS

1 (28-ounce) can **stewed tomatoes**
1 cup **corn kernels**, frozen or freshly cut from the cob
1 (15-ounce) can **black beans**, drained and rinsed
1 to 2 **jalapeños**, ribs and seeds removed, sliced (optional)
½ pound **orzo**
4 **scallions**, green and white parts, thinly sliced
2 cups blue or red **corn tortilla chips**, for garnish
1 **lime**, cut in wedges

INSTRUCTIONS

Follow the instructions for Quick Traditional Chicken Noodle Soup, adding the stewed tomatoes, corn, beans, and jalapeños if using along with the stock. Bring the soup back to a boil, stir in the orzo, and cook for 3 minutes. Stir in the chicken and cook for 5 to 6 minutes more to cook the chicken. Discard the bay leaf.

Ladle the soup into bowls and garnish with sliced scallions and tortilla chips. Serve with lime wedges to add zip.

SERVES 6

it's all in the numbers

VARIATION: Chicken Noodle Soup Italian Style

2   cups of the **chicken stock** (use 6 cups total)
    Egg noodles
    Dill
    Garnishes

1   (8-ounce) can **tomato sauce**
1   (15-ounce) can **kidney beans**, drained and rinsed
1   (15-ounce) can **chickpeas**, drained and rinsed
½   pound **whole-wheat penne** or other ridged pasta
2   cups **Parmesan pita chips**, for garnish (optional)
    Grated **Parmigiano-Reggiano cheese**, a handful

INSTRUCTIONS

Prepare the soup as for Quick Traditional Chicken Noodle Soup (page 98), adding the tomato sauce, kidney beans, and chickpeas. Bring the soup to a boil, stir in the penne, and cook for a minute or so. Stir in the chicken, reduce the heat, and simmer for 5 to 6 minutes more to cook the chicken. Discard the bay leaf.

Ladle the soup into bowls and garnish with some Parmesan pita chips, if using, and freshly grated Parmesan cheese.

SERVES 6

NIGHT 1: My Mom's Top-Secret Chicken Curry with Rice

This is a mild, sweet curry that's perfect for the whole family. My mom's secret ingredient (shh!) is mincemeat; she buys a large jar of Borden's Nonesuch Mincemeat, made with apples and raisins, and she keeps it in the freezer. One jar provides enough for a whole year!

INGREDIENTS

- 1 tablespoon EVOO (extra-virgin olive oil)
- 2 garlic cloves, chopped
- 1 onion, chopped
- 3 carrots, peeled and thinly sliced
- 4 celery ribs from the heart, chopped
- 3 cups chicken stock
- 3 boneless, skinless chicken breasts
- 5 to 6 boneless, skinless chicken thighs
- 1 bay leaf
- 1 cup basmati rice

> **THE ITTY BITTIES CAN:**
> - prep vegetables
> - shred poached chicken

MOM'S CURRY SAUCE

- 1 tablespoon EVOO (extra-virgin olive oil)
- 2 tablespoons butter
- 1 onion, chopped
- 2 garlic cloves, minced
  Salt
- 2 McIntosh apples, cored and chopped with skin on
- 1 tablespoon curry powder
- 2 tablespoons all-purpose flour
- 1 tablespoon peanut butter

2   tablespoons mincemeat

2   tablespoons Major Grey's or other mango chutney

2   teaspoons fresh lemon juice

TOPPINGS

Chopped scallions

Spanish peanuts

Unsweetened shredded coconut

Major Grey's chutney

INSTRUCTIONS

Poach the chicken: Heat the EVOO in a medium soup pot over medium to medium-high heat. Add the garlic, onions, carrots, and celery and sauté for 5 to 6 minutes to start to soften the vegetables. Add the chicken stock and 3 cups of water and bring to a boil, then reduce the heat to a simmer and add the chicken and bay leaf. Poach the chicken until cooked through, about 15 minutes, and turn off the heat.

In a saucepan combine the basmati rice with 2 cups of water. Bring to a boil, then reduce the heat to very low, cover, and cook for 20 minutes or until tender.

While the rice cooks, make the curry sauce. Heat the EVOO and butter together in a large skillet over medium heat. Cook the onions until they start to get really tender, then add the garlic and continue to cook until they caramelize, 12 to 15 minutes total. Next, add a little salt and the apples, and cook for 3 to 4 minutes. Sprinkle in the curry powder and flour, cook for 1 minute, then stir in the peanut butter, mincemeat, and chutney. Stir in about 2½ cups of the poaching liquid. Simmer the sauce for 5 minutes to combine the flavors while you chop and shred 2 of the poached chicken breasts and 2 to 3 of the poached chicken thighs. (Refrigerate the rest with the liquid and vegetables for Day 2.) Add the lemon juice to the sauce, turn off the heat, and fold in the shredded chicken.

Top shallow bowls of the chicken curry with a small scoop of rice and garnish with any or all of the toppings as you prefer.

SERVES 4

it's all in the numbers

NIGHT 2: Chicken Soup with Broken Spaghetti

Leftover **poaching liquid**, **poached chicken**, and **vegetables**

Salt and **freshly ground black pepper**

½ pound **whole-wheat spaghetti**, broken into 2- to 3-inch pieces

1 (15-ounce) can **red or white beans**, or chickpeas (optional)

Frozen chopped broccoli, spinach, or peas, defrosted and drained (optional)

Grated **cheese**, to pass at the table

> **THE ITTY BITTIES CAN:**
> * break spaghetti
> * drain vegetables
> * grate cheese

INSTRUCTIONS

Bring the refrigerated poaching liquid, chicken, and veggies to a boil over medium-high heat and season with salt and pepper to taste. Remove the chicken pieces and allow to cool. Meanwhile, stir in the pasta and simmer until it is al dente, 6 to 7 minutes. When the chicken has cooled a bit, chop it into bite-sized pieces and return them to the soup pot. The soup is great as is, or you can pump up the volume and vitamins by adding the beans or frozen veggies, or both. Heat through and serve. Pass a little cheese at the table for topping each serving of soup.

SERVES 4

everything soup

SUBMITTED BY AMY R. AND HER DAUGHTER CALISTA
(AGE TEN) FROM SKILLMAN, NEW JERSEY

This recipe was inspired by Rach's Italian Alphabet Soup, but Calista wanted to add even MORE stuff to it.

3 tablespoons EVOO (extra-virgin olive oil) • 1 pound lean ground beef • 1 small onion, chopped • 2 garlic cloves, smashed • 1 cup tomato or marinara sauce • 5 cups chicken stock • 1 cup alphabet pasta • 1 chunk of rind from Parmigiano-Reggiano cheese • 1 cup frozen peas and carrots or 1 cup frozen mixed vegetables • Salt and freshly ground black pepper

Heat 1 tablespoon of the EVOO in a medium skillet over medium-high heat. Add the ground beef and half of the chopped onions to the pan and cook for 6 to 7 minutes, or until browned. Transfer to a paper-towel-lined plate to drain.

In a medium soup pot, heat 2 tablespoons of the EVOO over medium heat. Add the garlic and the remaining onions and cook, stirring now and then, for 2 or 3 minutes. Stir in the tomato sauce, then slowly pour in the chicken stock. Bring the soup to a boil, then stir in the pasta and cheese rind. Reduce the heat to medium-low and simmer until the pasta letters are just tender, 6 to 7 minutes. Two or three minutes before the pasta is done, add the vegetables of your choice, a little salt and pepper, and the ground meat. Cool a few spoonfuls of soup and check the taste to see if it needs extra pepper or a little salt. Discard the cheese rind and serve.

SERVES 4

TUNA TWO TIMES

Two new takes on the good ol' Tuna Casserole—hold the canned condensed soup, please! Try a French twist on creamy tuna and egg noodles, or go Italian with a spicy tuna-tomato spaghetti. Serve either with a green salad for a super tuna supper.

Creamy Tuna with Tarragon and Egg Noodles

INGREDIENTS

Salt

¾	pound	**extra-wide egg noodles**
1	tablespoon	**EVOO** (extra-virgin olive oil)
1	small	**onion** or 1 large shallot, finely chopped
2	tablespoons	**butter**
2	tablespoons	**all-purpose flour**
1½	cups	**chicken stock**
½	cup	**half-and-half** or whole milk
1	tablespoon	**Dijon mustard**

Leaves from 3 to 4 **tarragon sprigs**, chopped

2 (6-ounce) cans **tuna in water**, drained and flaked with a fork

1 cup **frozen peas**, thawed

Freshly ground black pepper

1 slice **whole-wheat bread**

THE ITTY BITTIES CAN:

- drain tuna and flake
- make bread crumbs

INSTRUCTIONS

Bring a large pot of salted water to a boil over high heat. Add the egg noodles and cook al dente; they should still have a little bite left to them.

While you are waiting for the water to come to a boil, heat the EVOO in a large skillet over medium heat. Add the onions or shallots to the oil and cook for 3 to

YUM-O! the family cookbook

106

4 minutes, then add the butter to the pan. Once the butter has melted, sprinkle in the flour and stir, letting the butter-flour mixture cook for about 1 minute. Whisk in the stock and cook until it thickens, about 5 minutes. Add the half-and-half or milk and the mustard and bring the mixture back up to a bubble. Turn to low and add the tarragon, tuna, and peas. Mix well. Season the sauce with salt and pepper to taste.

Place the bread slice in a food processor and grind into medium crumbs. In a dry skillet, toast the crumbs until browned and crunchy.

Drain the noodles and combine with the sauce. Adjust the seasonings, top with the crumbs, and serve.

SERVES 4

it's all in the numbers

Spicy Tomato and Tuna Spaghetti

This spaghetti is topped with anchovy bread crumbs. In my family, we use these bread crumbs in place of grated cheese on just about any pasta made with fish. If you think you don't like anchovies, give this a shot: once they are heated through and cooked down, they taste like salted nuts. Believe me, these bread crumbs are really tasty!

INGREDIENTS

Salt

1	pound **whole-wheat spaghetti**
5	tablespoons **EVOO** (extra-virgin olive oil)
4	**garlic cloves**, grated or finely chopped
2	teaspoons **anchovy paste** (optional)
1	cup **Italian bread crumbs**
	A generous handful of **fresh flat-leaf parsley**, chopped
1	small **onion**, finely chopped
½	to 1 teaspoon **red pepper flakes**, or to taste
2	(6-ounce) cans **tuna in water**, drained
1	(28-ounce) can **Italian plum tomatoes** with their juices
	Freshly ground black pepper

THE ITTY BITTIES CAN:

- drain and flake tuna
- crush tomatoes

INSTRUCTIONS

Place a large pot of salted water over high heat and bring to a boil. Add the spaghetti and cook al dente.

While the water is coming to a boil, place a medium skillet with 3 tablespoons of the EVOO over medium heat. Add the garlic and anchovy paste, if using, and cook for a minute, then stir in the bread crumbs and cook and stir until they are toasted a deep golden brown. Stir in the parsley and remove from the heat.

Preheat a large skillet over medium heat with the remaining 2 tablespoons of EVOO. Add the onions and red pepper flakes, and cook until the onions are tender, about 5 minutes. Add the tuna and flake it with a fork, combining it with the onions. Add the tomatoes to the tuna and crush them with a potato masher. Let the tuna-tomato mixture cook for 5 to 6 minutes, then season with salt and pepper.

Drain the pasta and toss it with the tuna sauce. Sprinkle with the seasoned bread-crumb mixture for extra texture and great flavor.

SERVES 4

GRILLED EGGPLANT—THREE WAYS

A friend at work was having a baby and she LOVES eggplant so I came up with these three easy meals using eggplant steaks for her. I love you, Mommel Hommel, as much as you love eggplant. Enjoy!

Take 1: Chicken—Eggplant Steak Roll-up Salad

INGREDIENTS

About ½ cup **EVOO** (extra-virgin olive oil)

1 medium-large **eggplant**, sliced lengthwise into 8 steaks

Salt and **freshly ground black pepper**

4 **jarred roasted red peppers**, drained

2 tablespoons **balsamic vinegar**

2 cups shredded **rotisserie chicken**

8 marinated **bocconcini** (mozzarella balls), chopped (optional)

1 cup **basil**, about 20 leaves, chopped

1 **heart of romaine**, chopped

Juice of ½ **lemon**

THE ITTY BITTIES CAN:

- shred chicken
- puree dressing
- roll up eggplant

INSTRUCTIONS

Preheat a barbecue grill or grill pan to medium-high heat.

Pour ¼ cup of the EVOO into a small bowl. Brush the eggplant slices with the EVOO and season liberally with salt and pepper. Grill the eggplants for 3 to 4 minutes on each side and remove.

(recipe continues)

Meanwhile, in a food processor puree the roasted red peppers with the balsamic vinegar, about 3 tablespoons of the EVOO, and salt and pepper. Pour the dressing over the shredded chicken in a medium bowl. Toss to combine and add the chopped marinated cheese, if using.

Mound some chicken onto the narrow end of each eggplant slice, and then top each slice with lots of chopped basil. Roll up the eggplant from the narrower end to the wide, rounded end.

In a large mixing bowl toss the chopped romaine with the lemon juice, the remaining 1 tablespoon of EVOO, and salt and pepper.

Serve 2 roll-ups on a bed of dressed romaine per serving.

SERVES 4

Take 2: Eggplant Steak Lasagna Stacks

INGREDIENTS

- ⅓ cup plus 2 tablespoons EVOO (extra-virgin olive oil)
- 2 medium-large eggplants sliced into 6 steaks each
  Salt and freshly ground black pepper
- 1 onion, finely chopped
- 3 to 4 garlic cloves, chopped
- 1 (28-ounce) can diced or crushed fire-roasted tomatoes
  A handful of fresh basil leaves, torn
- 1½ cups ricotta
- ½ cup grated Parmigiano-Reggiano
- 1 egg yolk
  Nutmeg to taste
- 8 thin slices of smoked mozzarella (optional)

THE ITTY BITTIES CAN:

- slice eggplant
- tear basil
- layer lasagna stacks

Preheat a barbecue grill or grill pan to medium-high heat. Preheat the oven to 350°F.

Pour ⅓ cup of the EVOO into a small dish. Brush the eggplant steaks lightly on both sides with the oil and season with salt and pepper. Grill the steaks for 3 to 4 minutes on each side. You want the eggplant steaks a little undercooked. Transfer the grilled eggplant steaks to a platter in a single layer.

Heat the remaining 2 tablespoons of EVOO in a skillet over medium-high heat. Add the onions and garlic and sauté until translucent, 2 to 3 minutes. Add the tomatoes and their juices and the basil, stir, and simmer for 3 or 4 minutes.

Combine the ricotta, Parmigiano, egg yolk, and nutmeg in a bowl. Season with salt and pepper.

Build four lasagna stacks using 1 eggplant steak, ¼ cup cheese filling, sauce, eggplant steak, ¼ cup cheese filling, eggplant steak, and sauce. Lay 2 slices of mozzarella on top, if using. Arrange the stacks in a small baking pan.

Roast the stacks for 15 minutes or so, until heated through.

SERVES 4

Take 3: Meat and Mushroom Eggplant Roll-ups with Tomato Gravy

- ⅓ cup plus 3 tablespoons EVOO (extra-virgin olive oil)
- 2 medium-large eggplants sliced lengthwise into 6 steaks each
  Salt and freshly ground black pepper
- 1 pound ground meatloaf mix (beef, pork, and veal)
- ½ pound mushrooms such as cremini and shiitake, sliced
- 3 to 4 garlic cloves, chopped
- 2 fresh rosemary sprigs, chopped
- 2 slices whole-grain bread
- 3 tablespoons softened butter
- 2 tablespoons all-purpose flour
- 1 tablespoon tomato paste
- 3 cups beef stock
- ½ cup grated Parmigiano-Reggiano cheese, a couple of handfuls (optional)

> **THE ITTY BITTIES CAN:**
> - make bread crumbs
> - roll up eggplant

INSTRUCTIONS

Preheat a barbecue grill or grill pan to medium-high heat.

Pour ⅓ cup of the EVOO into a small dish. Brush the eggplant steaks lightly on both sides with the oil and season with salt and pepper. Grill the steaks for 3 to 4 minutes on each side and remove. You may need to prepare the steaks in batches. Transfer the grilled eggplant steaks to a platter and do not pile the eggplant up, as stacking hot eggplant will cause it to overcook.

Preheat a large nonstick skillet over medium-high heat with the remaining 3 tablespoons EVOO, three times around the pan, and add the ground meat. Break up the meat with the back of a spoon or wooden spatula and cook for 2 to 3 minutes. Add the mushrooms, garlic, and rosemary, reduce the heat a bit, and cook for 10 minutes, stirring frequently. Season with salt and pepper.

Meanwhile, toast the bread and butter it lightly with 1 tablespoon of the butter. Grind the bread into crumbs in the food processor or chop it by hand.

Melt the remaining 2 tablespoons of butter in a small sauce pot over medium heat. Whisk in the flour and cook for 1 minute. Whisk in the tomato paste, then 2 cups of the beef stock. Season with salt and pepper and reduce over low heat for 2 to 3 minutes.

Stir the bread crumbs into the meat and mushroom mixture and moisten with the remaining 1 cup stock. Mix in the cheese, if using.

Divide the meat and mushroom mixture among the 12 slices of eggplant. Roll up the eggplant around the mixture from the narrower end to the wide, rounded end.

Serve 3 eggplant roll-ups per person and top with gravy.

SERVES 4

Dinner Time!

People are always asking me what the best thing is for a family to have for dinner. My answer is . . . each other! Spending time together cooking, eating, remembering the events of the day—even sharing the cleanup duties—are my very favorite family memories and why and how I got interested in food and cooking as a job and a way of life. And what a life it's given me! Kids love to eat food that they've helped make, and most parents I know would love an extra hand in the kitchen after a long day; so get in there and cook together. There are lots of tasks even little kids can do, from grating cheese to peeling carrots or stirring up a sauce, and, hey, who knows? Maybe someday they'll end up with their own TV show. In any event, you'll all end up stars when you put any of these great, family-friendly thirty-minute meals on the table.

So eat together. Share food, stories, and your love for one another. With work, school, and everyone's crowded schedules it may not be possible to sit together every night, but any time you can it's priceless.

MENU

Inside-Out Turkey Bacon Cheeseburger with Oven O-Rings

Turkey Meatball Pocket Subs with Side Salad

BBQ Chicken Sloppy Joes with Pickled Slaw Salad

Awesome Autumn Stew

Tomato-Vegetable-Pasta Stoup

Ratatouille Stoup

Cacciatore Stoup with Turkey Sausage Meatballs

Clam Bake Stoup

Pepper and Onion Stoup with Chicken Sausages and Sun-Dried Tomato-Basil Gobble-Ums

Greek Goulash

Dracula's Transylvanian Ghoul-ash

Ground Meat Goulash with Macaroni

Buffalo Chicken Chili

Giant Chicken Tost-achos

Turkey Shepherd's Pie

Turkey Chili Dog Chili and Corny Corn Bread

Livia's Hot Dog-Pasta-Broccoli Bake

Not-Your-Mama's Tuna Salad

Eat-Your-Veggies Harvest Whole-Wheat Pasta

That's Shallota Flavor Spaghetti

Shrimp and Shells with Pancetta and Peas

More Peas If You Please Penne

Veggie P-schetti

Penne-Wise Pumpkin Pasta

Que Pasta Mexican Mac-n-Cheese

Whole Wheat Mac-n-Cheese for the Family

Sorta-Soba Noodle Bowls

Chinese Spaghetti and Meatballs

Farmer's Stack Pancake Supper

Tortilla and Tomato Toast

Pressed Manchego Cheese Sammies and Spicy Salad

Super-Size Egg Rolls with Mandarin Salad

Pretzel-Crusted Chicken Fingers and Zucchini Sticks with Cheddar-Spicy Mustard Dipping Sauce

"Everything" Chicken Fingers

Mega Turkey Nacho Dinner

Antip-achos: Italian Nachos and Fish Stick Parm

Lightened-Up Lemony Chinese Chicken

Sukiyaki Stir-fry

Not-Fried Chicken on the Ranch and Peeler Salad

Chicken Sausages with BBQ Butter Beans and Cheddar Cauliflower

Orange-Soy Pork Chops with Applesauce, Roast Potatoes and Green Beans

Inside-Out Sausage Chips with Roasted Peppers

Inside-Out Sausage Chops with Roasted Peppers

Turkey Sweet Potato Shepherd's Pie and Cran-Applesauce Sundaes

No-Thyme Quick Chicken with Smash Broc-o-tatoes and Gouda Gravy

Chicken with Apple Gravy, Cheesy Rice Pilaf with Peas, and Green Beans with Scallions

Pork Chops, Golden Apple and Raisin Sauce, and Whole-Wheat Pasta Mac-n-Cheddar with Broccoli

Paprika Pork Cutlets with Swiss Chard Egg Noodles

Spicy Spanish Shrimp, Cheesy Orzo, and Roasted Green Beans

Almond Snapper Fillets, Herb Rice with Peas and Carrots

Cornflake-Crusted Tilapia with Sweet and Spicy Watermelon Salsa

Inside-Out Turkey Bacon Cheeseburgers with Oven O-Rings

I made this for my friend Valerie Bertinelli, who is watching her figure but still cooking for her teenage rock-star son. This one deserves an encore; you'll make it twice a week!

INGREDIENTS

- 6 slices **turkey bacon**, chopped
- 1 tablespoon **EVOO** (extra-virgin olive oil)
- 1 cup **cornmeal**
- 1 teaspoon **smoked chipotle powder** or 2 teaspoons chili powder
  All-purpose flour, for dredging, about 1 cup
- 1½ cups **buttermilk**
- 1 large **sweet onion**, sliced ½ inch thick and divided into rings
- 2 pounds **ground turkey breast**
  Salt and **freshly ground black pepper**
- ¼ cup **spicy brown mustard**
- ¾ cup shredded or crumbled **sharp Cheddar cheese**
- ½ head of **redleaf or other lettuce**, chopped
- 1 **beefsteak tomato**, sliced
- 4 **kosher dill pickles**, chopped

> **THE ITTY BITTIES CAN:**
> - chop bacon
> - bread the onion rings
> - shred or crumble cheese

INSTRUCTIONS

Preheat the oven to 425°F.

Arrange the bacon in a large nonstick skillet and heat over medium heat. Slowly crisp up the bacon, cooking for 3 to 4 minutes on each side. Remove the bacon from the skillet and, when cool, chop. Add the EVOO to the remaining drippings and set aside.

While the bacon is crisping, combine the cornmeal and chipotle powder in a shallow bowl. Set up two more shallow bowls, filling one with the flour and the other with the buttermilk. Dip the onion rings in the buttermilk, then dredge the rings in the flour, tossing them lightly in your hands to remove the excess. Dip them once again in the buttermilk, and finally coat them fully with the cornmeal mixture. Place the dredged rings on a cookie sheet and bake until crispy, 15 to 18 minutes.

While the onion rings are baking, place the ground turkey in a large mixing bowl, season with salt and pepper, and mix in the mustard. Divide the meat into 4 equal portions. Shape each portion into a burger, making a well in the center. Fill the well of each with one quarter of the crisp bacon pieces and 2 tablespoons of the cheese. Carefully form the burger around the cheese and bacon filling, making sure the filling is completely covered. Return the skillet you cooked the bacon in to medium-high heat. Add the burger patties to the hot skillet and cook for 2 minutes on each side, then reduce the heat to medium-low and cook the burgers for 5 to 6 minutes longer, turning occasionally. Do not press down on the burgers as they cook.

Serve each burger on a bed of lettuce topped with sliced tomato, chopped pickles, and a few oven o-rings.

SERVES 4

Turkey Meatball Pocket Subs with Side Salad

3 slices stale whole-wheat bread (sandwich bread or crusty bread, whatever you have on hand)

½ to ⅔ cup milk

2 tablespoons EVOO (extra-virgin olive oil), twice around the pan, plus some for drizzling

1 large onion, peeled and quartered

3 garlic cloves, 1 crushed, 2 finely chopped

1 small carrot, peeled
Salt and freshly ground black pepper

1 cup chicken stock

1 (28-ounce) can crushed tomatoes

1 pound ground turkey breast
A handful of fresh flat-leaf parsley, finely chopped

¼ to ⅓ cup grated Parmigiano-Reggiano cheese, a generous handful

2 large whole-wheat pitas

1 small head of red or green leaf lettuce, washed and chopped

½ seedless cucumber, halved lengthwise, then thinly sliced into half moons

2 scallions, green and white parts, chopped

1 lemon

¼ cup basil leaves, a generous handful, chopped

4 thin slices fresh mozzarella cheese, halved

> **THE ITTY BITTIES CAN:**
>
> - tear bread slices and soak in milk
> - peel carrot
> - chop parsley
> - grate cheese
> - squeeze milk out of bread

Preheat the oven or toaster oven to 300°F to warm the pitas.

Chop or tear the stale bread into pieces and place in a bowl. Add enough milk to just barely cover, toss the bread pieces, and set aside to soak up the milk.

Heat the 2 tablespoons of EVOO in a deep skillet over medium heat. Once the oil is hot, grate three quarters of the onion into the pot. Add the crushed garlic, then grate and add the carrot. Season the vegetables with salt and pepper and cook, stirring frequently, for 5 minutes, or until the onions are tender. Stir in the chicken stock and the crushed tomatoes, bring the sauce up to a bubble, and simmer while you make the meatball mixture.

In a mixing bowl, grate the remaining onion quarter over the ground meat and add the parsley, the chopped garlic, the grated cheese, salt, and pepper. Squeeze the excess milk from the bread and add the bread to the meat mixture. Mix until just combined. Press the mixture into the bottom of the bowl, and score the meat into 4 equal portions with the side of your hand. Form each portion into 3 meatballs, dropping the meatballs into the bubbling sauce as you go. Shake and shimmy the meatballs in the sauce, cover the skillet with a lid or a piece of aluminum foil, and simmer the meatballs for 5 minutes. Uncover the pan and simmer for another 5 minutes, or until the meatballs feel firm and are cooked through.

While the meatballs are cooking away in the sauce, warm the pitas in the oven or toaster oven. Cut each one in half and spread the pocket open.

In a salad bowl, combine the lettuce, cucumber, and scallions. Squeeze the juice of the lemon over the greens and give it a good drizzle of EVOO. Season with a pinch of salt and some freshly ground black pepper and toss to combine.

Add the basil to the sauce and stir to combine, being careful not to break up the meatballs. Place 2 half moons of mozzarella cheese inside each pita pocket and top with 3 meatballs. Serve with a salad alongside.

SERVES 4

BBQ Chicken Sloppy Joes with Pickled Slaw Salad

I made this when Wayne Brady came by the show. He was so funny I could not speak! I do not think one person heard the recipe, so here it is, written down. He loved the joes. Maybe we should call 'em Sloppy Waynes. Nah. He dresses too spiffy for that name to stick!

INGREDIENTS

- 1 tablespoon EVOO (extra-virgin olive oil), once around the pan
- 2 pounds ground chicken
- 1 tablespoon grill seasoning, such as McCormick's Montreal Steak Seasoning
- 1 medium red onion, chopped
- 1 small red bell pepper, seeded and chopped
- 3 tablespoons red wine vinegar
- 3 tablespoons dark brown sugar
- 1 tablespoon Worcestershire sauce
- 1 (14-ounce) can tomato sauce
- 1 tablespoon hot sauce

THE ITTY BITTIES CAN:
- chop pickles
- toss salad

SLAW SALAD

- ⅓ cup pickle juice
- ¼ cup honey
- 2 tablespoons canola or vegetable oil
- 4 cups packed, shredded cabbage or packaged slaw mix (¾ pound)
  Salt and freshly ground black pepper

- 4 crusty rolls, split and toasted
- 1 cup chopped dill pickles

Make the sloppy joes: Heat the EVOO in a large nonstick skillet over medium-high heat. Add the ground chicken and use the back of a wooden spoon or spatula to break up the chicken into crumbles so it can brown evenly. Stir in the grill seasoning. Once the chicken begins to brown, 3 to 4 minutes, add the onions and bell peppers and cook for 5 to 6 minutes, until the vegetables begin to soften. In a bowl, combine the vinegar, brown sugar, Worcestershire, tomato sauce, and hot sauce. Stir the barbecue sauce into the chicken mixture. Reduce the heat to a simmer and let the mixture bubble for another 5 minutes.

For the slaw salad, in a large bowl combine the pickle juice (from the pickle jar) with the honey and canola or vegetable oil. Toss the cabbage with the dressing and season the slaw with salt and pepper.

Using a large spoon or ice cream scoop, pile the sloppy chicken onto toasted bun bottoms, then top with chopped pickles and the bun tops. Serve with the slaw salad.

SERVES 4

Awesome Autumn Stew

This pork stew is equally tasty made with boneless, skinless chicken thighs. Its savory-sweet flavor appeals especially to the little ones.

INGREDIENTS

- 2 **pork tenderloins** (about 1½ pounds)
  Salt and **freshly ground black pepper**
- 2 teaspoons **sweet paprika**
- ¼ cup **all-purpose flour**
- ¼ cup **EVOO** (extra-virgin olive oil)
- 1 large **onion**, cut in 1-inch dice
- 4 **carrots**, peeled and sliced ½ inch thick on an angle
- 5 to 6 **celery ribs** from the heart, sliced ½ inch thick on an angle
- 1 **bay leaf**
- 5 to 6 **fresh thyme sprigs**
- 4 **McIntosh apples**, quartered, cored, and cut into 1½-inch pieces
- 1 teaspoon **ground allspice**
- ½ cup **dried sweetened cranberries** (Craisins)
- 2 cups **apple cider (not apple juice)**
- 3 cups **chicken stock**
- 1 loaf crusty **whole-grain bread**

> **THE ITTY BITTIES CAN:**
> - measure ingredients
> - prep vegetables
> - line bowls with bread

INSTRUCTIONS

Trim the tenderloins, removing the shiny silver skin and connective tissue (or ask the butcher to do this for you). Cut the pork into 1½-inch pieces—big bites—and place the cubes on a rimmed baking sheet. Season the meat liberally with salt and pepper and toss with the paprika and flour until well coated.

Meanwhile, preheat a large heavy-bottomed pot over medium-high heat. Add the EVOO and once the oil ripples and begins to very lightly smoke, add the pork. Sear the meat until well browned on all sides, 7 to 8 minutes (lots of brown bits should be left in the bottom of the pot). Remove the meat to a platter and reserve.

Add the onions, carrots, celery, bay leaf, and thyme to the pot and season with salt and pepper. Cook the vegetables until they are beginning to become tender, 6 to 8 minutes. Add the apples, allspice, and cranberries and continue to sauté until the vegetables are quite tender but the apples still have some snap, 3 to 4 more minutes. Pour in the cider and use a wooden spoon to scrape up the brown bits that are stuck to the bottom of the pot. Add the chicken stock and toss the pork back into the pot. Bring the stew to a boil and simmer for 8 to 10 minutes or until the juices are slightly thickened, the cranberries have plumped, and the apples are tender. Pull out the bay leaf and thyme sprigs and discard them.

Line the bottom of six dinner bowls with a few chunks of bread. Ladle the stew on top of the bread and enjoy!

SERVES 6

Tomato-Vegetable-Pasta Stoup

- 2 tablespoons **EVOO** (extra-virgin olive oil)
- 1 **zucchini**, grated with the large holes of a box grater
- 2 **carrots**, peeled and grated
- 1 **onion**, chopped
- 4 **celery ribs**, chopped
- 1 **bay leaf**
  Salt and **freshly ground black pepper**
- 1 (15-ounce) can **chickpeas**, drained
- 2 jarred **roasted red peppers**, chopped
- 1 (28-ounce) can **crushed tomatoes**
- 4 cups (1 quart) vegetable or **chicken stock**
- ½ pound **whole-wheat penne pasta**
- ¼ cup storebought **pesto**

> **THE ITTY BITTIES CAN:**
> - grate zucchini and carrots
> - drain beans

INSTRUCTIONS

Heat a soup pot over medium-high heat with the EVOO. Add the zucchini, carrots, onions, celery, bay leaf, salt, and pepper and cook for 7 to 8 minutes. Stir in the chickpeas, red peppers, tomatoes, and stock and place a lid on the pot to bring to a boil. Add the pasta and cook to al dente, 6 to 7 minutes. Turn off the heat and stir in the pesto. Taste to adjust your seasonings, remove the bay leaf, and serve. Yum-o! If the stoup gets too thick, stir in a little water.

SERVES 4

Ratatouille Stoup

If you loved Remy the rat chef in the movie *Ratatouille,* then you're bound to love this healthy, hearty soup that shares the same name. C'est magnifique!

- 3 tablespoons EVOO (extra-virgin olive oil), 3 times around the pan
- 1 medium onion, chopped
- 3 garlic cloves, chopped
- 1 green bell pepper, seeded and diced
- 1 red bell pepper, seeded and diced
- 1 medium eggplant, peeled and diced
- 2 small zucchini, diced
  Salt and freshly ground black pepper
- 3 to 4 sprigs fresh thyme
- 1 (28-ounce) can diced tomatoes with their juices
- 6 cups (1½ quarts) chicken stock
- ½ pound small cut whole-wheat pasta
  A handful of fresh flat-leaf parsley, finely chopped
  A few fresh basil leaves, torn or shredded

> THE ITTY BITTIES CAN:
> - dice zucchini
> - tear basil

INSTRUCTIONS

Heat the EVOO in a deep pot over medium-high heat. Add the onions, garlic, bell peppers, eggplant, and zucchini. Season the vegetables with salt, pepper, and thyme and cook until softened, about 7 to 8 minutes, stirring now and then. Add the tomatoes and chicken stock and bring the soup to a boil, then reduce it to a simmer. Stir in the pasta and cook al dente. Stir in the parsley and basil, adjust the salt and pepper, and serve.

SERVES 6

dinner time!

Cacciatore Stoup with Turkey Sausage Meatballs

Cacciatore originally was a slow-cooked hunter's stew of rabbit and wild mushrooms that has morphed into a spicy on-the-bone chicken dish with vegetables and tomato sauce. Here it gets a fast, fun update that the whole family will love! Plus, it's easy cleanup for whoever gets stuck with the dishes!

INGREDIENTS

- 3 tablespoons EVOO (extra-virgin olive oil), 3 times around the pan
- 2 portobello mushroom caps, wiped clean, chopped into bite-size cubes
- 2 cubanelle peppers (light green, mild Italian peppers), seeded and chopped into bite-size pieces
- 1 large red bell pepper, seeded and chopped into bite-size pieces
- 1 large onion, coarsely chopped
- ½ to 1 teaspoon red pepper flakes, depending on how spicy you like your food
  Coarse salt and black pepper
- 3 slices crusty whole-grain bread
- ½ cup milk
- 1 pound ground turkey breast
- 1 egg
- ½ cup grated Parmigiano-Reggiano or Romano cheese, a couple of handfuls, plus more to pass at the table
  A handful of fresh flat-leaf parsley, finely chopped
- 2 garlic cloves, finely chopped
- 1 (28-ounce) can San Marzano tomatoes or canned whole plum tomatoes of your choice
- 4 cups (1 quart) chicken stock
  Crusty whole-grain bread, to pass at the table

THE ITTY BITTIES CAN:

- clean and chop mushrooms
- rip up bread
- form meatballs

Heat the EVOO in a Dutch oven or soup pot over medium-high heat. Add the portobello mushrooms, peppers, and onions and cook until tender, 7 to 8 minutes. Season the vegetables with red pepper flakes, salt, and black pepper.

While the vegetables cook, rip up the 3 slices of bread and place them in a mixing bowl with the milk to soak for 5 minutes. Add the turkey, egg, cheese, parsley, garlic, and salt and pepper to the bowl. Mix to combine.

Add the tomatoes to the pot and break up with a wooden spoon, then stir in the stock and raise the heat to bring the mixture to a boil. When the stoup boils, form 2-inch meatballs with the turkey mixture and drop into the stoup. Cover the pot, reduce the heat, and simmer the meatballs in the stoup for 10 to 12 minutes, until the meatballs are cooked through. Serve in shallow bowls with the remaining bread for mopping and extra cheese for topping.

SERVES 4

Clam Bake Stoup

All the flavor of a clambake—without the sand!

- 2 tablespoons **EVOO** (extra-virgin olive oil)
- ¾ pound turkey or regular **kielbasa**, diced
- 4 cups frozen **diced hash browns** (half of a 32-ounce bag)
- 1 large **onion**, chopped
- 4 **celery ribs**, chopped
- 1 **bay leaf**
- 5 to 6 **fresh thyme sprigs**
  Salt and **freshly ground black pepper**
- 2 pounds **large shrimp**, peeled and deveined
- 1 rounded tablespoon **seafood seasoning**, such as Old Bay, a generous palmful
  Kernels from 4 large **ears of corn** or 3 cups frozen kernels
- 1 (15-ounce) can **diced fire-roasted tomatoes** with their juices
- 4 cups (1 quart) **chicken stock**
- 4 dozen **littleneck clams**
  Hot sauce
  Zest and juice of 1 lemon
  A handful of **fresh flat-leaf parsley**, chopped
- 4 jumbo **sourdough English muffins**, split
- 1 **garlic clove**, peeled and halved
- 3 tablespoons softened **butter**
- 2 tablespoons chopped **fresh chives**

> **THE ITTY BITTIES CAN:**
>
> - zest and juice lemon
> - peel garlic
> - rub toasted muffins with garlic

Heat a large soup pot with the EVOO over medium-high heat. Add the kielbasa and brown for 2 minutes, then add the hash browns, onions, celery, bay leaf, thyme, salt, and pepper. Sauté and let the veggies soften up, stirring occasionally, for 10 minutes.

(recipe continues)

Pat the shrimp dry and season by tossing in a bowl with the seafood seasoning.

Add the corn, tomatoes, and stock to the pot and cover to bring up to a boil, 4 to 5 minutes. Add the shrimp and clams and replace the lid. Cook until the shrimp are pink and firm and the clams have opened, 5 to 6 minutes. Stir in hot sauce to taste, the lemon zest and juice, and the parsley.

While the stoup cooks, toast the English muffins. Rub the hot toasted muffins with the cut sides of the garlic, then butter the muffins and sprinkle with the chives. Chop the muffins into large dice.

Serve the stoup in shallow bowls topped with the muffin croutons. Place an extra bowl at each place to collect the clam shells.

Yum-o!

SERVES 6

TIDBIT

To cut the kernels off an ear of corn without making a big mess, invert a small bowl and place in a large bowl. Shuck the corn and stand one ear on end on the small bowl. Use a large, sharp knife to slice off the kernels. They will fall within the large bowl.

italian chili soup

SUBMITTED BY DEE DEE O. AND HER DAUGHTER EMMA JOY
(AGE SIX) FROM HUMBLE, TEXAS

Dee Dee and her family double this recipe so they can eat it as a snack the next day, for lunch, and for dinner. Now *that's* getting a good bang for your buck.

Salt • ½ box of ditalini pasta, or any short pasta, whole-wheat or regular • 1 tablespoon EVOO (extra-virgin olive oil) • 1 pound lean ground beef • Freshly ground black pepper • 3 celery ribs, diced • 1 cup grated carrots • 1 onion, diced • 2 garlic cloves, chopped • 1½ teaspoons garlic salt • 1½ teaspoons dried basil • 1½ teaspoons dried oregano • ¾ teaspoon dried thyme • 1 (15-ounce) can white beans, undrained • 1 (15-ounce) can kidney beans, undrained • 1 (28-ounce) can petite diced tomatoes with juice • 1 (15-ounce) can tomato sauce • 1 (15-ounce) can original vegetable cocktail, such as V-8 • 1 tablespoon white vinegar • 1 cup shredded mozzarella cheese, for garnish

Place a large pot of salted water over high heat for the pasta. Cook the pasta according to the package instructions. Drain.

While the pasta water is coming to a boil, heat the EVOO in a large sauce pot over medium-high heat. Add the ground beef, season with salt and pepper, and cook for 5 to 6 minutes, breaking the meat up with a wooden spoon. When the meat is browned, add the celery, carrots, onions, and garlic and cook for 10 minutes, or until the veggies lose some of their crunch. Add the garlic salt, basil, oregano, and thyme and cook for a minute, then add the white beans, kidney beans, diced tomatoes, tomato sauce, V-8 juice, and vinegar. Cook for 5 to 10 minutes, or until the flavors come together.

To serve, place some of the pasta in the bottom of a bowl. Ladle some chili soup on top and sprinkle with mozzarella cheese.

SERVES 4

Pepper and Onion Stoup with Chicken Sausages and Sun-Dried Tomato–Basil Gobble-Ums

Braised sausages in a thick pepper and onion soup with cubed sun-dried-tomato and basil garlic bread on top: serious yum-o! Serve with a tossed green salad dressed with oil and vinegar.

INGREDIENTS

- 8 fresh chicken sausages or packaged chicken sausages in an Italian or Mediterranean flavor
- 4 tablespoons EVOO (extra-virgin olive oil)
- 1 large onion, quartered lengthwise then thinly sliced
- 2 cubanelle peppers, seeded and thinly sliced
- 2 red bell peppers, seeded, quartered lengthwise, and thinly sliced
- 4 to 5 cups frozen shredded potatoes
  Salt and freshly ground black pepper
- 1 (28-ounce) can chunky-style crushed or diced tomatoes
- 4 cups (1 quart) chicken stock
- 2 garlic cloves, grated
- 4 tablespoons (½ stick) softened butter
- 3 to 4 tablespoons sun-dried tomato paste
- 1 cup fresh basil leaves, about 20 leaves, thinly sliced
- ¼ cup grated Parmigiano-Reggiano cheese, plus some to pass at the table
- ½ loaf good-quality Italian bread or a long crusty loaf of whole-grain bread, split lengthwise

THE ITTY BITTIES CAN:

- mix tomato-basil spread
- slather spread on bread

Preheat the oven to 425°F.

In a large skillet with high sides, arrange the sausages and add about ½ inch water and a healthy drizzle of EVOO, about 1 tablespoon. Place the sausages over medium-high heat, allow the liquids to come to a boil and evaporate, then rotate the sausages to crisp the casings, 18 to 20 minutes total. You'll need a little less water and the process will go faster for fully cooked packaged chicken sausage.

While the sausages cook, heat a medium soup pot over medium-high heat with the remaining 3 tablespoons EVOO. Add the onions, peppers, and potatoes, season with salt and pepper, and sauté for 7 to 8 minutes, or until the onions and peppers begin to soften and the potatoes become lightly golden at the edges. Stir in the tomatoes and chicken stock and bring the stoup to a bubble, then reduce the heat to a simmer over medium-low. If the stoup is too thick, add some water to thin it out a bit to your taste. The consistency should be between that of a soup and a stew.

Combine the garlic, butter, sun-dried tomato paste, basil, and cheese in a medium bowl. Slather the bread with the spread and cube it into large bite-size pieces. Arrange the Gobble-Ums on a baking sheet and roast for 5 to 7 minutes, until toasted.

Slice the sausages and divide the slices among 6 soup bowls. Ladle the stoup over the sausage. Top with a few cubes of bread. Serve hot.

SERVES 6

Greek Goulash

Salt

6 pita breads

Olive oil cooking spray

2 tablespoons EVOO (extra-virgin olive oil), twice around the pan

1 pound ground sirloin or lamb

Black pepper

1 teaspoon dried oregano or 2 fresh oregano sprigs, finely chopped

2 pinches of ground cinnamon

1 onion, chopped

4 garlic cloves, grated

1 small eggplant, peeled and chopped into ¼-inch dice

1 (10-ounce) box frozen spinach, defrosted and wrung dry in a clean kitchen towel

1 (15-ounce) can tomato sauce

½ pound orzo

½ cup kalamata black olives, pitted

Zest of 1 lemon

½ cup fresh flat-leaf parsley leaves, a couple of handfuls

¾ cup feta cheese crumbles

> **THE ITTY BITTIES CAN:**
> - cut pitas
> - squeeze spinach dry
> - sprinkle cheese

INSTRUCTIONS

Preheat the oven to 400°F. Bring a large pot of water to a boil for the orzo and salt it generously.

Cut the pita rounds into 6 wedges each with a knife or kitchen scissors. Scatter the wedges onto a baking sheet and spray with olive oil cooking spray. Season with salt and bake for 10 minutes, or until golden. Cool.

Heat the EVOO in a large deep skillet over medium-high heat until the oil ripples. Add the beef or lamb and cook, breaking up the meat with a wooden spoon, until browned and crumbled, about 5 minutes. Season the meat with salt, pepper, oregano, and cinnamon. Add the onions, garlic, and eggplant and cook for 6 to 7 minutes, then stir in the spinach and tomato sauce. Simmer for a few minutes and adjust the seasonings.

While the goulash simmers, cook the orzo in the boiling water until it is al dente.

On a cutting board, chop the olives together with the lemon zest and parsley to make Greek gremolata!

Drain the orzo and stir it into the goulash mixture. Serve bowls of goulash topped with some feta cheese and pita chips and a sprinkling of the olive gremolata.

Opa!

SERVES 4

Dracula's Transylvanian Ghoul-ash

This is garlicky enough to keep the most persistent of vampires off your doorstep. One bite and you'll want to nuzzle up to this ghoul-ash any night of the week. Serve with some wilted spinach on the side.

INGREDIENTS

- 1 pound **sirloin steak**
  Salt
- 1 pound **extra-large egg noodles**
- 4 tablespoons (½ stick) **butter**
- 3 to 4 tablespoons chopped **fresh dill**
- 3 to 4 tablespoons chopped **fresh chives**, about 20 chives
- 2 tablespoons **EVOO** (extra-virgin olive oil)
  Freshly ground black pepper
- ½ cup **all-purpose flour** (eyeball it), for dusting the steak
- ½ small **onion**, peeled
- 4 to 5 **garlic cloves**, peeled
- 2 teaspoons **smoked paprika**
- 1 (4-ounce) jar **chopped pimientos**, thoroughly drained
- 2 cups **beef stock**
- ½ cup **sour cream**

> THE ITTY
> BITTIES CAN:
>
> - snip chives
>   with scissors
> - peel garlic
> - toss noodles
>   with butter and
>   herbs

(recipe continues)

Place the steak in the freezer for about 10 minutes, remove, and slice the meat against the grain as thin as you can manage (the slices should be the size of the egg noodles).

Place a large pot of water over high heat and bring to a boil. Once it is boiling, add salt and the egg noodles and cook al dente. Drain the noodles, return to the hot pot, and toss with 2 tablespoons of the butter and half of the dill and chives; stir to combine.

When the water is close to a boil, place a large skillet over medium-high heat with the remaining 2 tablespoons of butter and the EVOO. While the skillet is heating up, season the steak slices with salt and pepper, then toss with the flour to coat evenly. Add the coated sliced steak to the skillet, spread out in an even layer. Brown the meat for 2 to 3 minutes alone, then grate the onion and garlic over the meat, sprinkle with the paprika, give the skillet a stir, and continue to cook for 2 to 3 minutes. Add the drained pimientos and the beef stock and stir to combine. Bring up to a bubble and simmer until lightly thickened, about 1 minute. Stir in the sour cream and give the meat a taste to see if it needs any more salt and pepper.

Divide the buttered herbed noodles among 4 plates, and top with ghoul-ash. Sprinkle with the remaining dill and chives.

SERVES 4

10 WHOLE-GRAIN FOODS TO TRY

Already upgraded to whole-grain sandwich bread and ready to get more whole grains on the menu? Try these:

- whole-grain pasta (penne, spaghetti, linguine)
- whole-wheat couscous
- whole-grain English muffins
- whole-wheat pitas
- rolled oats (not instant)
- whole-wheat or buckwheat pancake mix
- multi-grain crackers
- whole-wheat sandwich wraps and tortillas
- bulgur wheat (cook like rice and serve as you would couscous)
- whole-grain pretzels

Ground Meat Goulash with Macaroni

INGREDIENTS

Salt

1 pound **macaroni**

2 tablespoons **EVOO** (extra-virgin olive oil), twice around the pan

1½ pounds **ground beef, pork, and veal**, combined

1 tablespoon **sweet paprika**

Freshly ground black pepper

1 **bay leaf**

1 cup **shredded carrots**, chopped into small bites

1 **onion**, finely chopped

2 **celery ribs** from the heart, finely chopped

1 **red bell pepper**, seeded and finely chopped

1 (15-ounce) can **tomato sauce**

2 cups **beef stock**

½ cup **sour cream**

3 tablespoons chopped **fresh dill**

A handful of **fresh flat-leaf parsley**, finely chopped

3 tablespoons freshly snipped **chives**

4 **radishes**, finely chopped, for garnish

½ cup chopped **cornichons** or baby gherkin pickles, for garnish

Bring a large pot of water to a boil for the macaroni. Salt the water, then cook the pasta al dente.

While the water comes to a boil and the pasta cooks, heat the EVOO in a large, deep skillet over medium to medium-high heat. Add the meat and season with the paprika, salt, and pepper. Brown and crumble the meat for 5 minutes, then add the bay leaf, carrots, onions, celery, and bell pepper and cook for 10 minutes more. Add the tomato sauce and stock and heat through, about 2 minutes. Discard the bay leaf. Adjust the seasonings and stir in the sour cream, dill, and parsley. Drain the macaroni and toss with the meat sauce. Garnish the goulash with the chives, chopped radishes, and chopped pickles.

SERVES 4

Buffalo Chicken Chili

This was the most frequently downloaded recipe from the first 180 episodes of my daytime TV show, *Rachael Ray*. It really is too good to be good for you. You can make it with ground chicken, too, but here I've used chopped whole chicken breasts.

- 2 tablespoons EVOO (extra-virgin olive oil), twice around the pan
- 2 pounds ground chicken or chopped raw chicken
- 2 large carrots, peeled and finely chopped
- 1 large onion, chopped
- 4 celery ribs with leafy tops, finely chopped
- 4 garlic cloves, chopped
- 1 tablespoon sweet smoked paprika
- 1 bay leaf
  Salt and freshly ground black pepper
- 2 cups chicken stock
- ½ cup hot sauce, such as Frank's
- 1 (15-ounce) can tomato sauce
- 1 (15-ounce) can stewed or crushed fire-roasted tomatoes with their juices
- 1 (9 to 13-ounce) bag whole-grain tortilla chips, lightly crushed
- ¾ pound Maytag blue cheese, crumbled
  A handful of fresh flat-leaf parsley, chopped

> **THE ITTY BITTIES CAN:**
> - peel carrots
> - crush chips
> - crumble cheese and top chips

INSTRUCTIONS

Heat the EVOO in a large pot over medium-high heat. Add the chicken and cook until it's lightly browned, breaking it up with a wooden spoon as it cooks. Add the carrots, onions, celery, garlic, paprika, and bay leaf and season with salt and pepper. Cook, stirring frequently, for 7 to 8 minutes, then add the chicken stock and stir to scrape up any brown bits on the bottom of the pot. Add the hot sauce, tomato sauce, and the tomatoes and bring the chili up to a bubble. Simmer for 8 to 10 minutes more to bring the flavors together. Discard the bay leaf before serving.

While the chili is simmering, preheat the broiler. Spread the chips on a baking sheet and top with the crumbled blue cheese. Broil until the cheese melts, 2 to 3 minutes, then sprinkle with the chopped parsley.

Top each serving of chili with a few blue-cheese chips.

SERVES 6, OR 4 WITH SOME LEFTOVERS

Giant Chicken Tost-achos

A tostada is like a mega-nacho: a tortilla topped with beans or meat and cheese and veggies. Try this simple, fun Mexican-American meal with your family and friends. Each tost-acho is topped with chicken and taco sauce, cheese, and salad: Yum-olé!

EVOO (extra-virgin olive oil) to brush the tortillas

4 (6-inch) flour, whole wheat, or spinach tortillas

2 cups chopped or shredded rotisserie chicken meat

1 cup mild taco sauce or salsa

2 cups shredded Monterey Jack or Cheddar

1 small heart of romaine, shredded

2 scallions, white and green parts, chopped

4 rounded spoonfuls of sliced green olives with pimiento

> **THE ITTY BITTIES CAN:**
>
> - shred chicken
> - shred cheese and lettuce
> - assemble nachos

INSTRUCTIONS

Preheat the oven to 350°F. Lightly brush a little oil onto the tortillas and place them on a baking sheet. Place in the oven and crisp up the tortillas, about 5 minutes.

In a large skillet over medium heat, cook the chicken and taco sauce for 5 minutes, or until heated through.

Top each tortilla with ½ cup of the saucy chicken and lots of cheese. Place the hot baking sheet back in the oven and bake for 3 to 4 minutes more to melt the cheese.

Place each Giant Chicken Tost-acho on a dinner plate and top with lettuce, scallions, and olives.

SERVES 4

Turkey Shepherd's Pie

I love mashed potatoes because they taste great and because they are so much fun to smash up! In shepherd's pie the mashed potatoes serve as a crust, so the dish is traditionally called a pie even though it's technically not one. Make sure the kids are in there for the smashing; that's the key to the whole thing!

INGREDIENTS

- 4 large Idaho or russet potatoes (2½ to 3 pounds), peeled and cut into chunks
  Salt
- 2 tablespoons EVOO (extra-virgin olive oil), twice around the pan
- 2 slices bacon, chopped
- 2 pounds ground turkey or ground turkey breast
  Freshly ground black pepper
- 2 onions, chopped
- 2 carrots, peeled and chopped
- 2 tablespoons Worcestershire sauce (eyeball it)
- 2 teaspoons poultry seasoning
- ⅔ cup half-and-half or cream
- 1 egg, beaten
- 2 tablespoons butter, softened
- 2 tablespoons fresh chives, snipped or chopped
- 1 cup frozen peas
- 1 teaspoon paprika

THE ITTY BITTIES CAN:

- peel carrots
- mash potatoes

INSTRUCTIONS

Place the potatoes in a small deep pot with water to cover. Cover and bring to a boil over high heat. Salt the water and cook the potatoes until tender, 12 to 15 minutes.

While the potatoes cook, heat the EVOO in a deep skillet over medium-high to high heat. Add the bacon and cook until crisp, about 5 minutes, then add the turkey. Season the turkey with salt and pepper and brown it for 5 minutes, breaking it up with a wooden spoon, then push it to the sides of the pan and add the onions and carrots to the center of the pan. Season the veggies with salt and pepper and let them cook where it is hottest for 5 minutes, then mix everything together. Add the Worcestershire sauce and poultry seasoning, then turn the heat down to medium and cover the pan with a foil tent to keep in some of the moisture. Cook for another 6 to 7 minutes.

Preheat the broiler to high.

Drain the potatoes and place back in the warm pot. Use a pot holder to steady the pot while you smash the potatoes. Add ⅓ cup of the half-and-half, the egg, butter, and chives and smash away with a masher until the potatoes are almost smooth but still a little lumpy. Season with salt and pepper.

Uncover the turkey mixture and stir in the peas and the remaining ⅓ cup of half-and-half. Scrape up any good bits from the bottom of the pan and turn off the heat. Scrape the turkey mixture into a casserole dish and top with a thick layer of smashed potatoes. Brown the potatoes under the broiler for a few minutes, sprinkle with the paprika, and serve.

SERVES 6

Turkey Chili Dog Chili and Corny Corn Bread

My young friend Livia Lange should change her name to Lovia Hot Dog Lange because man, does she love hot dogs! These next two recipes are for her. This one is a mix-up of chili dogs and corn dogs with mustard. We use lean ground turkey and turkey dogs, but vegetarian kids could use tempeh and tofu dogs.

INGREDIENTS

- 2 (8.5-ounce) boxes **corn bread mix**, such as Jiffy (you'll need 2 eggs and ⅔ cup of milk to prepare the mix)
- 2 cups **frozen corn kernels**, thawed
- 2 tablespoons **spicy brown mustard** (eyeball it)
  Nonstick cooking spray
- 2 tablespoons **EVOO** (extra-virgin olive oil)
- 1 (16-ounce) package **turkey hot dogs**, cut into bite-size pieces
- 2 pounds **lean ground turkey**
- 2 medium **onions**, chopped (reserve ¼ of 1 onion and finely chop)
- 4 **garlic cloves**, minced or grated
- 2 **jalapeño peppers**, seeded and finely chopped
- 2 tablespoons **chili powder**, 2 palmfuls
- 1 tablespoon **ground cumin**, about a palmful
  Salt and **freshly ground black pepper**
- 1 (28-ounce) can **diced fire-roasted tomatoes** (or any diced tomatoes you like)
- 1 (15-ounce) can **red kidney beans** (or another type of small red bean), drained
- 2 to 3 cups **chicken or beef stock**, as needed
  Hot sauce
  Shredded **sharp Cheddar** or smoked Cheddar, to pass at the table
  Veggie sticks, to pass at the table

> **THE ITTY BITTIES CAN:**
> - mix corn bread
> - cut turkey dogs
> - grate cheese

Preheat the oven and prepare the corn bread according to the package directions. Fold in the corn kernels and spicy brown mustard. Spray an 8 x 8-inch baking dish with cooking spray, pour in the batter, and bake as directed.

Place a large, deep pot over medium-high heat with 1 tablespoon of the EVOO, once around the pan. Add the chopped hot dogs and cook, stirring every now and then, until lightly browned, about 3 minutes. Remove the browned dogs to a bowl and add the remaining tablespoon of EVOO to the pan. When hot, add the ground turkey to the pot and use the back of a spoon or a potato masher to break up the meat while it cooks and browns, about 5 to 6 minutes. Once the meat is browned add the chopped onions, the garlic, jalapeños, chili powder, cumin, salt, and pepper. Cook until the onions start to get tender, about 5 minutes. Add the tomatoes, beans, reserved hot dogs, and stock. Season with hot sauce to taste, bring up to a bubble, and simmer for 10 minutes.

Serve up the chili topped with shredded Cheddar and the reserved finely chopped onion; offer veggie sticks and a chunk of the corny corn bread alongside.

SERVES 6

Livia's Hot Dog–Pasta–Broccoli Bake

Livia Lange and her mom, Terry, came up with this recipe idea on an airplane, where we all dream about good food.

INGREDIENTS

- 1 pound short cut **whole-wheat pasta**, such as penne or shells
- 1 head of **broccoli**, chopped into florets
  Salt
- 2 tablespoons **EVOO** (extra-virgin olive oil)
- 1 package **turkey hot dogs**, chopped into bite-size pieces
- 2 to 3 **garlic cloves**, chopped
  Freshly ground black pepper
- 1½ cups grated **Parmigiano-Reggiano cheese**

> **THE ITTY BITTIES CAN:**
> - chop broccoli into florets
> - chop turkey dogs
> - grate cheese
> - toss pasta

INSTRUCTIONS

Heat a large pot of water for the pasta and a skillet with 2 inches water for the broccoli. Salt the water in both pans. Cook the pasta al dente and the broccoli 4 to 5 minutes until tender. Reserve 1 cup of starchy pasta water before draining the pasta, then drain both the broccoli and the pasta.

Preheat the broiler.

When the broccoli is done, heat the EVOO in a large, deep ovenproof skillet over medium heat. Lightly brown the dogs for 3 to 4 minutes, then add the broccoli and garlic and sauté for 1 to 2 minutes. Add the reserved starchy cooking liquid from the pasta and the pasta to the pan. Season the pasta and broccoli with salt and pepper and toss with half the cheese. Sprinkle the remaining cheese on top and slide the skillet under the broiler to brown the top, 3 to 4 minutes.

SERVES 4 TO 6

BUILDING A BETTER (SALAD) BOWL

I don't know how many recipes I've written that end with "Serve with a green salad." The truth is, I don't always have time to make a separate veggie dish; many nights dinner at my house (and probably yours, too) consists of pasta, a sandwich, or a bowl of soup with a salad on the side. Why not make that salad count by choosing add-ons that pack the most nutritional punch—and by going easy on those with higher fat content? Here are some basic guidelines:

GOOD

sliced radishes
sliced cucumbers
chopped celery
bean sprouts
Belgian endive
sliced fennel
onions and scallions

BETTER

shredded carrots
cooked or raw green beans
cooked or raw beets
chopped apples and pears
dried fruit such as Craisins or apricots
canned beans
thawed peas or edamame
avocado
shredded red cabbage
snow peas

BEST

chopped tomatoes
cubed baked tofu
chopped green and red bell peppers
   (more than just a sliver or two)
citrus segments

NOT SO MUCH (USE SPARINGLY)

bacon bits
crumbled or shredded cheese
croutons
mayo-based dressings
marinated artichoke hearts
nuts, sunflower or other seeds (a
   tablespoon or two, chopped, is
   fine)

Not-Your-Mama's Tuna Salad

This yum-o! pasta salad can even go to the beach with you because it is made without mayo, which can spoil if it's not kept really cold. This salad also makes a fun and easy cold supper on warm summer nights.

Salt

1 pound medium **pasta shells**

1 cup **store-bought pesto**

Juice of 1 lemon

2 (6-ounce) cans **tuna in water**, drained

4 **scallions**, green and white parts, chopped

1 whole **roasted red pepper**, chopped

A handful of **grape tomatoes**, halved

Freshly ground black pepper

THE ITTY
BITTIES CAN:

• juice lemon
• flake tuna

INSTRUCTIONS

Bring a large pot of water to a boil. Salt it generously, then add the pasta and cook al dente. Drain the pasta, then run under cold water to cool the pasta. Drain again.

Place the pesto in a bowl and stir in the lemon juice. Add the tuna to the bowl and break it up with a fork. Add the scallions, red pepper, tomatoes, and pasta to the bowl, then toss to coat the salad with the dressing. Season with salt and pepper to taste.

SERVES 4

chick chick veggie pasta

SUBMITTED BY DEBBY D. AND DAUGHTER MEGAN (AGE ELEVEN) FROM SACRAMENTO, CA

This pasta recipe was sent to us by Debby and her daughter, Megan. Little Meg helps with the chopping and grating of veggies as well as during cleanup time. What a great kid!

1 pound whole-wheat spaghetti or penne • ½ red onion, thinly sliced • 1 red bell pepper, seeded and sliced • 2 cups sliced mushrooms • 1 cup shredded carrots • 1 cup shredded zucchini • 2 tablespoons EVOO (extra virgin olive oil) • 1 cup frozen peas • 2 garlic cloves, sliced • Salt and freshly ground black pepper • 1 teaspoon red pepper flakes • Zest and juice of 2 lemons • 2 grilled chicken breasts, sliced • ½ cup grated Parmigiano-Reggiano cheese • ¼ cup chopped fresh flat-leaf parsley

Cook the pasta according to package instructions.

While the pasta cooks, sauté the onions, bell peppers, mushrooms, carrots, and zucchini in the EVOO for 5 minutes. Add the peas, garlic, salt, black pepper, red pepper flakes, and lemon juice.

Drain the pasta, reserving ½ cup of the pasta water. Add the pasta, pasta water, and sliced chicken to the veggies and cook for 3 minutes more, or until heated through. Serve topped with the grated cheese, lemon zest, and parsley.

SERVES 4 TO 6

Eat-Your-Veggies Harvest Whole-Wheat Pasta

Whether you have a garden or just a great farmers' market in town, this dish really celebrates the flavor and goodness of vegetables. It's a hearty meal that tastes too good to be so good for you.

INGREDIENTS

Salt

1	pound whole-wheat penne
4	small or 2 medium zucchini, cut in ½-inch dice
1	medium yellow squash or 1 small eggplant, cut in ½-inch dice
1	red bell pepper, seeded and cut in ½-inch dice
1	red onion, cut in ½-inch dice
¼	cup plus 3 tablespoons EVOO (extra-virgin olive oil)

Freshly ground black pepper

¼	cup sliced almonds, toasted
1	cup fresh basil, about 20 leaves
¾	cup fresh flat-leaf parsley, 3 handfuls of leaves
¼	cup fresh mint leaves, a generous handful
1	garlic clove
½	cup grated Parmigiano-Reggiano cheese, a couple of handfuls
1	cup ricotta cheese

Freshly grated or ground nutmeg

> **THE ITTY BITTIES CAN:**
> - pull leaves from herb stems
> - grate cheese

INSTRUCTIONS

Preheat the oven to 400°F.

Bring a large pot of water to a boil over high heat for the pasta. Once it reaches a boil, add salt and the pasta and cook until al dente. Heads-up: you will need to reserve a cup of starchy cooking liquid just before you drain the pasta.

While the pasta is cooking, place the zucchini, yellow squash, bell pepper, and red onion on a rimmed baking sheet. Drizzle about 3 tablespoons of the EVOO over the vegetables and season with salt and pepper. Roast for about 15 minutes or until tender and golden brown.

While the vegetables are roasting, place the almonds, herbs, and garlic in a food processor. Pulse the processor while drizzling in the ¼ cup of EVOO. Transfer the herb mixture to a large mixing bowl and stir in the grated cheese.

In a small mixing bowl, combine the ricotta cheese, a little freshly ground black pepper, and nutmeg to taste; set aside.

Stir the reserved cup of cooking water into the herb paste. Toss the pasta with the roasted veggies and sauce and adjust the seasoning. Serve the pasta topped with a dollop of the ricotta cheese to stir in.

SERVES 6

That's Shallota Flavor Spaghetti

I make this *all the time*; it's a real knockout and an absolute *fave*! Made with ten shallots per pound of whole-wheat spaghetti, it's like a bowl of French onion soup, hold the broth. Serve it with a spinach or arugula salad on the side for a simple supper any night.

- ¼ cup **EVOO** (extra-virgin olive oil), 4 times around the pan
- 2 **garlic cloves**, finely chopped
- 10 **shallots**, halved then thinly sliced
  Salt and **freshly ground black pepper**
- 1 pound **whole-wheat spaghetti**
  A generous handful of **fresh flat-leaf parsley**, chopped
- 1 cup grated **Parmigiano-Reggiano cheese**

> **THE ITTY BITTIES CAN:**
> - chop parsley
> - sprinkle cheese

INSTRUCTIONS

Heat the EVOO over medium-low heat in a deep skillet. Add the garlic and shallots, season with salt and pepper, then gently cook for 20 minutes to caramelize them, stirring occasionally.

Meanwhile bring a large pot of water to a boil for the pasta. Salt the water very liberally, then add the spaghetti and cook al dente. Just before you drain the pasta, add 3 ladles of the starchy pasta cooking water, about 1¼ cups, to the shallots and stir. Drain the pasta and add to the skillet with the shallots. Add the parsley and cheese and more black pepper to taste. Toss over medium heat for 1 to 2 minutes to allow the liquid to absorb into the pasta, then serve. Wow! Talk about yum-o!

SERVES 4

Shrimp and Shells with Pancetta and Peas

Shrimp and pasta sea shells? This one is as cute as it is tasty and simple. Peas and bacon or pancetta have been a favorite of mine since I was little. Adding protein and pasta turns an old, favorite side dish into a main course.

INGREDIENTS

Salt

- 1 pound **medium-size pasta shells**
- 2 tablespoons **EVOO** (extra-virgin olive oil)
- ¼ pound **pancetta**, chopped, or 4 slices bacon, chopped
- 1 medium **onion**, chopped
- 3 to 4 **garlic cloves**, chopped or grated
- 1 pound **medium shrimp**, peeled and deveined, tails off

Freshly ground black pepper

- 2 (10-ounce) boxes **frozen peas**, defrosted
- 1 teaspoon grated **lemon zest**

Juice of ½ lemon

- 2 cups **chicken stock**
- ¼ cup packed **fresh flat-leaf parsley** leaves, a couple of handfuls

> **THE ITTY BITTIES CAN:**
>
> - puree peas in processor
> - zest lemon
> - pull leaves from parsley stems

INSTRUCTIONS

Bring a large pot of water to a boil over high heat. Salt the water, add the pasta shells, and cook al dente, with a bite left to it. Drain and reserve.

While the pasta is cooking, place a large nonstick skillet over medium-high heat and add the EVOO, twice around the pan. Add the pancetta and cook for 3 to 4 minutes, or until browned. Add the onions and garlic and cook for 3 to 4 minutes.

Add the shrimp and cook for 5 to 6 minutes, until the shrimp are pink and firm. Season the mixture with salt and pepper.

While the pancetta and shrimp are cooking, place half of the defrosted peas in a food processor along with the lemon zest, lemon juice, and 1 cup of the chicken stock. Puree until smooth.

Add the pea puree to the skillet along with the remaining cup of chicken stock to thin it out; add the parsley and the reserved peas. Season the shrimp and pea mixture with salt and pepper. Add the cooked pasta shells and toss to combine, then serve.

SERVES 4, WITH SMALL SECONDS FOR SOME

More Peas If You Please Penne

Penne gets its name from the Latin word for *quill* or *feather*. It looks like the sharpened tip of an old-fashioned quill pen. Enjoy these "pens" with peas and cheese!

Salt

1 pound **penne pasta with ridges** (penne rigate)

3 cups **frozen peas**

½ cup **chicken or vegetable stock**

2 cups **ricotta cheese**

3 tablespoons **butter**, cut into small pieces

1 cup grated **Parmigiano-Reggiano cheese**
Freshly ground black pepper

1 cup **fresh basil leaves**, torn or shredded

THE ITTY BITTIES CAN:

- mash peas with ricotta
- grate cheese
- tear basil leaves
- toss pasta

INSTRUCTIONS

Bring a large pot of water to a boil over high heat for the pasta. Once it reaches a boil, add salt and the pasta and cook al dente.

While the pasta is cooking, place the peas and stock in a small pot and simmer for 5 minutes.

Spoon half of the peas and a little hot pasta water into a large shallow dish and mash the peas with the ricotta cheese. Drain the pasta and add to the bowl with the mashed peas and ricotta. Add the butter and half of the Parmigiano-Reggiano, toss to combine, and season with salt and pepper. Add the remaining whole peas and adjust the salt and pepper. Top with the remaining cheese and garnish with basil. Pea-rfect!

SERVES 4

Veggie P-schetti

This recipe is a wholesome, whole-grain, positively veggie-packed version of pasta primavera.

INGREDIENTS

Salt

- 1 pound **whole-wheat spaghetti**
- ¼ cup **EVOO** (extra-virgin olive oil), 4 times around the pan
- 1 **red onion**, quartered and thinly sliced
- 2 medium **zucchini**, trimmed, halved, sliced lengthwise, and cut into matchsticks
- 2 medium **yellow squash**, trimmed, halved, sliced lengthwise, and cut into matchsticks
- 2 cups store-bought **shredded carrots**
- 3 large **garlic cloves**, finely chopped or grated
  Freshly ground black pepper
- 1 **red bell pepper**, seeded and thinly sliced into matchsticks
- 1 cup grated **Parmigiano-Reggiano cheese**, plus more to pass at the table
- 1 cup shredded **fresh basil leaves**

> **THE ITTY BITTIES CAN:**
>
> - halve, slice, and cut zucchini and yellow squash
> - shred basil leaves

INSTRUCTIONS

Place a large pot of water over high heat and bring to a boil. Salt the water, add the pasta, and cook al dente. Heads-up: you will need to reserve 1 cup of the pasta cooking liquid right before draining.

Heat the EVOO in a large skillet over medium-high heat. Add the onions, zucchini, and yellow squash to the skillet. Add the carrots and garlic, season with salt and pepper, and sauté for 5 minutes. Add the bell pepper and cook for 3 to 4 minutes more. Stir in the reserved pasta cooking liquid and bring up to a bubble. Add the drained pasta, the grated cheese, and the basil and toss for 1 minute to combine and blend the flavors.

SERVES 4 TO 6

Penne-Wise Pumpkin Pasta

This recipe is "wise" because it uses whole-wheat pasta, which is high in protein and fiber compared with semolina pasta. Plus, it's inexpensive to make and absolutely delicious!

Salt

1 pound whole-wheat penne pasta

2 tablespoons EVOO (extra-virgin olive oil)

3 shallots, finely chopped

3 to 4 garlic cloves, grated

2 cups chicken stock

1 (15-ounce) can pumpkin puree

½ cup cream

1 teaspoon hot sauce, or to taste

Freshly grated or ground nutmeg

2 pinches of ground cinnamon

Freshly ground black pepper

7 to 8 fresh sage leaves, thinly sliced

Grated Parmigiano-Reggiano cheese

INSTRUCTIONS

Bring a large pot of water to a boil over high heat for the pasta. Add salt and the pasta and cook al dente, reserving ½ cup of the starchy pasta water.

In a large skillet, heat the EVOO, twice around the pan, over medium heat. Add the shallots and garlic to the pan and sauté for 3 minutes. Stir in the chicken stock, pumpkin, and cream, then season the sauce with the hot sauce, nutmeg, cinnamon, salt, and pepper. Reduce the heat to medium-low and simmer for 5 to 6 minutes longer to thicken. Add a little of the reserved pasta water if needed to thin out the sauce a bit. Stir in the sage, then toss in the drained pasta and grated cheese.

SERVES 6

Que Pasta Mexican Mac-n-Cheese

- 4 **poblano peppers**
  Salt
- 1 pound **farfalle** (bow-tie pasta) or whole-wheat penne
- 1 tablespoon **EVOO** (extra-virgin olive oil)
- 1 **onion**, finely chopped
- 2 **garlic cloves**, grated or finely chopped
- 2 tablespoons **butter**
- 2 tablespoons **all-purpose flour**
- 1 cup **chicken stock**
- 2 cups **milk**
  Freshly ground black pepper
- 1½ teaspoons **ground cumin**, ½ palmful
- 1½ teaspoons **ground coriander**, ½ palmful
- 2½ cups **grated Mexican cheese blend** or mix of Cheddar and queso fresco or Chihuahua cheeses
- 1 firm **avocado**, diced
  Juice of 1 lime
- 2 small **vine-ripe tomatoes**, seeded and chopped
- 4 **scallions**, green and white parts, chopped

THE ITTY BITTIES CAN:

- grate cheese
- dice avocado
- juice lime

INSTRUCTIONS

Heat the broiler to high and blacken the poblanos on all sides, 12 to 15 minutes. Place the peppers in a bowl and cover tightly with plastic wrap or place in a paper sack; cool for 10 minutes, then peel, seed, and chop.

Bring a large pot of water to a boil for the pasta. Add salt and the pasta and cook al dente.

Heat a sauce pot over medium heat; add the EVOO, onions, and garlic and cook until tender, 6 to 7 minutes. Add the butter to the pan and when it melts, stir in the flour and cook for 1 minute. Whisk in the stock and milk and bring to a simmer.

Season with salt, pepper, the cumin, and the coriander and cook until thickened, about 5 minutes. Stir in the cheese with a wooden spoon in a figure-eight pattern until the cheese melts.

Drain the pasta and toss with the sauce and the chopped poblano peppers. Toss the avocado with the lime juice. Serve the mac-n-cheese in shallow bowls and top with the tomatoes, avocados, and scallions.

SERVES 4 WITH SECONDS

chickenadas

SUBMITTED BY KATHRYN P. AND HER DAUGHTER ANNABETH
(AGE TEN) FROM JACKSONVILLE BEACH, FLORIDA

2 tablespoons EVOO (extra-virgin olive oil) • ½ small onion, finely chopped • ½ red bell pepper, seeded and finely chopped • 2 garlic cloves, minced • 2 cups chopped cooked chicken • 1 tablespoon chili powder • Salt and freshly ground black pepper • 5 ounces cream cheese, softened • 1 cup shredded Cheddar cheese • 1 package refrigerated pie crust • Nonstick cooking spray

Preheat the oven to 400°F.

Heat the EVOO in a small sauté pan over medium-high heat. Add the onions, bell peppers, and garlic and cook until soft, 4 to 5 minutes. Add the chopped chicken, chili powder, salt, and pepper and cook for 3 to 4 minutes, or until heated through; transfer to a mixing bowl. Stir in the cream cheese and Cheddar cheese.

Using a 3-inch round cookie cutter or drinking glass, cut out rounds from the pie crust. Place a tablespoon or so of the mixture in the center of each pastry round. Brush the edges with water, fold the dough over, and seal the edges with a fork. Spray the tops with cooking spray and place on a greased cookie sheet. Bake the empanadas until they are brown, 15 to 20 minutes. Serve plain or with salsa for dipping.

SERVES 4 TO 6

Whole-Wheat Mac-n-Cheese for the Family

The secret ingredient in this mac-n-cheese is Dijon mustard.

INGREDIENTS

2	tablespoons **butter**
2	tablespoons **all-purpose flour**
1	cup **chicken stock**
1½	cups **milk**
2	cups grated **sharp Cheddar cheese**
	Salt and **freshly ground black pepper**
1	tablespoon **Dijon mustard**
1	pound **whole-wheat pasta**, cooked al dente and drained
1	head of **cauliflower**, cut into florets and steamed until almost tender, 6 to 7 minutes

THE ITTY BITTIES CAN:

- grate cheese
- break cauliflower into florets

INSTRUCTIONS

In a sauce pot, melt the butter over medium-low heat, add the flour, and cook for 1 minute. Whisk in the chicken stock and milk. Thicken the sauce for 5 minutes, then stir in the cheese, season with salt and pepper, and stir in the secret ingredient (the mustard).

Toss the sauce with the whole-wheat pasta and cauliflower. Yum-o!

SERVES 4 TO 6

Sorta-Soba Noodle Bowls

Soba are the buckwheat noodles used in Japanese cooking, but not every grocery store stocks them. I use whole-wheat spaghetti for this easy Japanese-inspired noodle-veggie-shrimp stir-fry, and it's pretty close to the real thing.

INGREDIENTS

Salt

1 pound whole-wheat spaghetti

2 tablespoons canola oil, twice around the pan

1 pound medium shrimp, peeled and deveined, tails off

4 scallions, green and white parts, cut into 2-inch pieces

2 handfuls of string beans, about ½ pound, trimmed and cut lengthwise into strips

1 red bell pepper, seeded and cut into strips

1 green bell pepper, seeded and cut into strips

3 garlic cloves, chopped

½ cup orange marmalade

¼ cup tamari or soy sauce

½ cup chicken stock

2 teaspoons hot sauce

Freshly ground black pepper

1 tablespoon toasted sesame seeds, for garnish (optional)

> THE ITTY BITTIES CAN:
> - trim beans
> - combine ingredients for sauce

INSTRUCTIONS

Bring a large pot of water to a boil over high heat for the pasta. Once it reaches a boil, add salt and the pasta and cook al dente.

Place a large skillet over high heat and add the canola oil. When hot, add the shrimp and vegetables and stir-fry for 4 to 5 minutes, or until the shrimp are pink and firm.

While the vegetables are cooking, in a medium mixing bowl whisk together the marmalade, tamari, chicken stock, hot sauce, and some freshly ground black pepper.

Drain the pasta and toss it with all the ingredients in the skillet. Pour the sauce over the contents of the pan and toss to combine. Taste for seasoning and adjust flavors if needed: you can add a splash more stock, tamari, or hot sauce to taste. Garnish with toasted sesame seeds, if desired.

SERVES 4

Chinese Spaghetti and Meatballs

INGREDIENTS

Salt

1 pound whole-wheat spaghetti

1 pound ground pork or chicken

1 egg

2 cups puffed rice cereal

Black pepper

1 teaspoon Chinese five-spice powder, ⅓ palmful

8 scallions, green and white parts, 2 finely chopped, 6 cut into 2-inch lengths

2 tablespoons plus ⅓ cup tamari or soy sauce

3 tablespoons vegetable oil

2 cups snow peas, sliced thin on an angle

1 red bell pepper, seeded and very thinly sliced

2-inch piece of fresh ginger, peeled and grated

4 garlic cloves, grated

1 pound triple-washed spinach, heavy stems removed, coarsely chopped

1 tablespoon toasted sesame oil, available on the Asian foods aisle

3 tablespoons toasted sesame seeds, available on the Asian foods aisle

INSTRUCTIONS

Preheat the oven to 375°F.

Place a large pot of water on to boil for the spaghetti. When it comes to a boil, salt the water, add the pasta, and cook al dente. Heads-up: you'll need to reserve ½ cup of the pasta cooking water just before draining.

Place the pork in a mixing bowl. Add the egg and combine. Place the rice cereal in a food processor and pulse until the cereal has the consistency of bread crumbs.

Add the cereal crumbs to the bowl along with salt and pepper to taste, the five-spice powder, the finely chopped scallions, and 2 tablespoons of the tamari. Mix thoroughly. Form the seasoned meat mixture into 1½-inch balls and scatter on a rimmed baking sheet. Drizzle the meatballs with 1 tablespoon of the vegetable oil and roll around to coat, then roast for 15 minutes.

When the meatballs are close to done and the pasta is working, heat a large skillet over high heat with the remaining 2 tablespoons of vegetable oil. Add the snow peas, bell pepper, the cut scallions, the ginger, and the garlic and stir-fry for 2 minutes. Add the spinach and toss until it wilts, 1 minute. Add the remaining ⅓ cup tamari and the sesame oil. Add the drained pasta and the reserved pasta cooking water and toss to combine so the pasta can soak up the sauce, 1 minute. Garnish with the sesame seeds and top with lots of meatballs.

SERVES 4

worms and toes

SUBMITTED BY CHANA R. AND HER DAUGHTER ANAYA
(AGE FIVE) FROM GRANGER, INDIANA

Chana cooks this recipe for her three kids, Anaya, Creed, and Kale. Two of them are diabetic, so she uses whole-wheat pasta.

1 pound whole-wheat spaghetti • 1 tablespoon EVOO (extra-virgin olive oil) • 1 (12-ounce) package regular or turkey kielbasa • 1 bunch of asparagus, trimmed and cut into 2-inch pieces • 1 (15-ounce) can stewed tomatoes • 2 tablespoons pesto

Cook the pasta according to the instructions on the package.

While the pasta is cooking, heat the EVOO in a large skillet over medium-high heat. Cook the sausage until heated through. Cut the sausage in half lengthwise, then crosswise in ½-inch pieces. (These are the toes.) Return the sausage pieces to the pan and add the asparagus. Sauté for 2 or 3 minutes, then add the stewed tomatoes and pesto to the pan and cook for another 2 minutes. Add the cooked pasta to the pan and toss to combine. Enjoy your yummy worms and toes!

SERVES 4

Farmers' Stack Pancake Supper

8   slices **turkey bacon**

2   ripe **pears**, such as Bartlett or Bosc, peeled, cored, and chopped

4   McIntosh, Honey Crisp, Gala, or Golden Delicious **apples**, peeled, cored, and chopped

1   cup unfiltered, all-natural **apple cider** (eyeball it)

1   **cinnamon stick**

1   cup plus 2 tablespoons **pure maple syrup** (eyeball it)

1   pound **ground turkey breast**

1   tablespoon **grill seasoning**, about a palmful

1   teaspoon **fennel seeds**, about ⅓ palmful

1   teaspoon **poultry seasoning**, about ⅓ palmful

2   tablespoons **EVOO** (extra-virgin olive oil)

1   tablespoon **butter**

     Buckwheat pancake mix, prepared according to the package directions to yield 12 pancakes

4   **eggs**

> **THE ITTY BITTIES CAN:**
> - form sausage patties
> - mix batter

INSTRUCTIONS

Preheat the oven to 375°F. Bake the bacon until crisp, about 10 minutes. Remove and reserve. Reduce the oven temperature to warm.

Place the pears, apples, cider, and cinnamon stick in a large pot and bring to a boil, then reduce the heat to medium and cook until a chunky sauce forms, 12 to 15 minutes. Stir in the cup of maple syrup and remove the cinnamon stick. Cover the pot and keep it warm over low heat until ready to serve.

While the sauce is simmering, combine the ground meat with the remaining 2 tablespoons of maple syrup, the grill seasoning, fennel seeds, and poultry seasoning. Form 4 large, thin patties.

Heat 1 tablespoon of the EVOO in a large nonstick skillet over medium-high heat. Add the patties and cook for 5 minutes on each side, or until cooked through.

While the turkey sausage patties are cooking, heat a griddle pan or nonstick skillet over medium heat. Nest the butter into a folded paper towel and rub a touch of butter across the hot skillet. Cook twelve 4-inch buckwheat pancakes, buttering the skillet between batches as needed. Keep warm in the low oven as you complete them.

Place a medium skillet over medium-high heat with the remaining tablespoon of EVOO. Cook the eggs over medium heat any way you like them.

Stack 1 turkey sausage patty, 1 pancake, 1 egg, 1 pancake, 2 strips of bacon, and 1 more pancake on each of 4 plates. Spoon a hearty helping of pear-apple-maple sauce over the top and serve 'em up!

SERVES 4

Tortilla and Tomato Toast

You don't use these tortillas to make a quesadilla or to roll up a burrito. In Spain tortillas are egg pies—like a big flat omelet. They are cooked in olive oil and they are delish! My fave is a potato tortilla served with *chapata* (toasted bread with tomato smushed all over). You can make and eat this yum-o meal for breakfast, lunch, or dinner! Olé!

INGREDIENTS

- ¼ cup EVOO (extra-virgin olive oil), plus some for drizzling
- 2 potatoes, peeled and thinly sliced
- 1 onion, peeled and thinly sliced
- Salt
- 8 eggs
- ¼ cup whole milk
- 8 slices crusty bread
- 2 really ripe tomatoes

THE ITTY BITTIES CAN:

- peel potatoes
- whisk eggs
- rub tomato on bread

INSTRUCTIONS

Heat the EVOO in a medium skillet over medium heat. Add the potatoes and onions and salt them. Cook the potatoes for about 15 minutes, turning them every 2 to 3 minutes. Try not to let the potatoes get brown; you just want them tender.

Preheat the broiler.

Whisk the eggs and milk in a large bowl and season with salt. Pour the eggs over the potatoes. Let the omelet settle and get firm at the edges, then place the skillet under the broiler and brown the top until the tortilla is firm and golden.

Remove the tortilla from the broiler and cool, leaving the broiler on.

Place the bread on a baking sheet and toast under the broiler. Cut the tomatoes in half and squish and rub their guts all over the toasted bread. Drizzle each slice with EVOO and season with salt. Cut the tortilla into 4 wedges and serve with the tomato bread.

SERVES 4

Pressed Manchego Cheese Sammies and Spicy Salad

INGREDIENTS

- 1 **garlic clove**, peeled
- 2 tablespoons **sherry vinegar** (eyeball it)
- 2 teaspoons **Dijon mustard**
- A few dashes of **hot sauce**
- Lots of **freshly ground black pepper**
- ⅓ cup plus 2 tablespoons **EVOO** (extra-virgin olive oil)
- 2 hearts of **romaine lettuce**, cleaned, dried, and chopped or torn
- ½ small **red onion**, thinly sliced
- **Salt**
- 3 tablespoons **capers**, drained
- A generous handful of **pitted green olives**, coarsely chopped
- A handful of **fresh flat-leaf parsley**, chopped
- ¼ cup **sliced toasted almonds**
- 8 slices **crusty bread**
- ¾ pound **Manchego cheese**, sliced
- 2 **piquillo peppers** or 1 roasted red pepper, chopped

THE ITTY BITTIES CAN:

- wash, dry, and tear lettuce
- chop olives

INSTRUCTIONS

Grate the garlic with a Microplane or on the small side of a box grater into the bottom of a large salad bowl. Add the sherry vinegar, mustard, hot sauce, and black pepper to the bowl, then whisk in about ⅓ cup of the EVOO in a slow stream. Add the lettuce and onions to the bowl and toss to coat. Season the salad with salt to taste. Top the salad with the capers, olives, parsley, and almonds.

Heat the remaining 2 tablespoons EVOO in a large nonstick skillet over medium heat until the oil is very hot.

Make 4 sandwiches of bread, Manchego cheese, and a sprinkle of chopped piquillo or roasted peppers. Press with a brick covered in foil or with a smaller skillet weighted with full cans. Press and griddle the sammies in the skillet until deeply golden and the cheese has melted, 5 to 6 minutes, turning once.

Cut the sammies in half and serve next to huge piles of the spicy Spanish salad.

SERVES 4

Supper-Size Egg Rolls

Filled with lots of veggies and baked not fried, these egg rolls are good and good for you! Swap out the pork for chopped shrimp, tofu, or ground chicken to mix it up.

INGREDIENTS

- 2 tablespoons canola oil
- ½ pound ground pork
- 2 small celery ribs from the heart, finely chopped
- A handful of shiitake mushroom caps, chopped
- ½ head of napa cabbage, shredded
- A handful of bean sprouts
- ¼ cup drained water chestnuts, chopped
- 2 garlic cloves, finely chopped
- 1-inch piece of fresh ginger, peeled and grated
- 1 egg
- 2 tablespoons tamari or soy sauce
- 16 (13 x 17-inch) sheets frozen phyllo dough, defrosted
- 3 to 4 tablespoons melted butter, for brushing the dough
- Duck sauce and/or Asian sweet-hot mustard, to pass at the table. This is a great use for those leftover packets of duck sauce or sweet-hot mustard from take-out orders.

> **THE ITTY BITTIES CAN:**
> - chop mushrooms
> - brush butter on pastry

INSTRUCTIONS

Place the oven rack in the center position and preheat the oven to 400°F.

Heat the canola oil in a large nonstick skillet over high heat. Add the pork and brown for 2 to 3 minutes, breaking it up with a wooden spoon as it cooks. Add the celery and mushrooms and stir-fry for 1 minute, then add the cabbage, bean sprouts, water chestnuts, garlic, and ginger. Stir-fry for 2 to 3 minutes more. Stir in the tamari, transfer to a bowl, and cool. Once the mixture is cool enough to handle, pour the egg over the mixture and combine. This will help the filling keep its shape when you bake the rolls.

Roll out one sheet of phyllo dough on a large work surface. Brush the entire sheet with a little melted butter, paying extra attention to the perimeter. Place another whole sheet of phyllo on top of the buttered surface and fold both sheets in half widthwise. Pile one eighth of the pork mixture onto the dough 2 inches from the bottom and from each side. Tuck the bottom up and fold both sides in, then roll and wrap upward to the top edge of the dough. Each pastry will resemble a large egg roll. Brush the seam and the ends of the roll with butter and set the roll seam side down on a baking sheet. Make 7 more rolls. Bake for 15 minutes or until lightly golden all over. Serve 2 per person.

SERVES 4

Mandarin Salad

INGREDIENTS

- 2 tablespoons **orange marmalade**
- 2 teaspoons **soy sauce**
- 1 tablespoon **rice wine vinegar** or white wine vinegar
- 3 tablespoons **canola oil**
- 2 hearts of **romaine lettuce**, chopped
- ½ cup **mandarin orange sections**, drained
  Salt and **freshly ground black pepper**

THE ITTY BITTIES CAN:

- make dressing ingredients
- chop lettuce
- drain orange sections

INSTRUCTIONS

In a salad bowl, whisk together the orange marmalade, soy sauce, and vinegar. Whisk in the oil. Add the lettuce and oranges and toss to coat with the dressing, then season with salt and pepper.

SERVES 4

Pretzel-Crusted Chicken Fingers and Zucchini Sticks with Cheddar–Spicy Mustard Dipping Sauce

The original recipe for Pretzel-Crusted Chicken, from *365: No Repeats,* remains one of the most popular meals of the literally thousands I've written in the last decade. Here, it rides again in that most kid-pleasing form: chicken fingers! I added zucchini sticks to the meal as well and swapped in whole-wheat pretzels for the regular kind.

INGREDIENTS

- 1 bag **whole-grain pretzels**, any shape
- 2 teaspoons **dried thyme** or 2 tablespoons fresh chopped thyme leaves
- 3 **eggs**
- 4 (6- to 8-ounce) **boneless, skinless chicken breasts**
- 2 medium **zucchini**, halved and cut into sticks
  Salt and **freshly ground black pepper**
  EVOO (extra-virgin olive oil), for frying
- 2 tablespoons **butter**
- 2 tablespoons **all-purpose flour**
- 1 cup **chicken stock**
- 1 cup **milk**
- 1½ to 2 cups shredded **sharp yellow Cheddar cheese**, 10 to 12 ounces
- 2 heaping tablespoons **spicy brown mustard**, such as Gulden's
- 2 large **carrots**, peeled and cut into ½ by 4-inch sticks
- 4 **celery ribs**, halved lengthwise and cut into 4-inch sticks
- 8 **dill pickle spears**

> THE ITTY
> BITTIES CAN:
>
> - crush pretzels
> - cut vegetables
> - bread chicken and zucchini
> - shred cheese

Preheat the oven to 250°F.

Place the pretzels in a plastic bag and using a rolling pin, crush the pretzels until fine. Transfer to a shallow dish and season with the thyme. Beat the eggs with about ½ cup water in a second shallow dish. Slice each chicken breast into 3 long strips, cutting into the breast on an angle. You should have 12 large chicken fingers. Season the chicken and zucchini sticks with salt and pepper. Coat the chicken breast and zucchini in the ground pretzels, then in egg, then in the pretzels again.

Heat just enough oil to coat the bottom of a large nonstick skillet over medium to medium-high heat. Cook the chicken in a single layer, in 2 batches if necessary, for about 3 minutes on each side, until the juices run clear and the breading is evenly browned. Drain the chicken on paper towels, then place in the oven on a baking sheet to keep warm while you cook the remaining chicken and zucchini, adding a little more oil to the skillet if necessary.

Melt the butter in a medium sauce pot over medium heat. Add the flour and cook for 1 minute, then whisk in the stock and milk. When the sauce comes to a bubble and thickens, stir in the cheese and mustard. Season with salt and pepper.

Serve the chicken and zucchini sticks with small bowls of the dipping sauce and with carrot sticks, celery sticks, and dill pickle spears on the side.

SERVES 4

"Everything" Chicken Fingers

Yup, here's another recipe for chicken fingers. This one is a riff on everything bagels (my favorite). With a vegetable cream cheese sauce for dipping, it's high-protein, low-carb fun!

INGREDIENTS

- 3 tablespoons dehydrated minced onion
- 3 tablespoons garlic flakes
- 3 tablespoons poppy seeds
- 3 tablespoons sesame seeds
- 2 tablespoons coarse black pepper
- 1 tablespoon coarse salt or sea salt
- 2 tablespoons EVOO (extra-virgin olive oil)
- 1½ pounds chicken tenders
- 1 (8-ounce) package cream cheese, softened
- 1 cup buttermilk
- 4 scallions, white and green parts, chopped
- 1 carrot, peeled and grated
- 2 celery ribs from the heart with leafy tops, finely chopped

> **THE ITTY BITTIES CAN:**
> - mix coating blend
> - peel carrots
> - stir dipping sauce

INSTRUCTIONS

Preheat the oven to 375°F.

Combine the minced onion, garlic flakes, poppy seeds, sesame seeds, black pepper, and coarse salt on a plate and toss with your fingers to mix. Drizzle the EVOO over the chicken tenders and toss to coat. Press the chicken pieces into the seed mixture to coat on all sides. Place the chicken on a nonstick baking sheet and bake for 20 to 25 minutes, turning once about halfway through.

Meanwhile, combine the cream cheese and buttermilk and stir until smooth. Stir in the scallions, carrots, and celery and season with a little salt and pepper.

Serve the chicken tenders with the scallion–cream cheese sauce alongside.

SERVES 4

TIPS FOR PICKY EATERS

My friends at the Alliance for a Healthier Generation passed along these smart ideas for getting your little ones to go for the good stuff:

- Get your kids excited about healthy food: Let them smell, touch, taste, ask questions and try fruits, veggies, yogurts, and other healthy foods in the kitchen. Ask them what they think of each and let them know their opinions count.
- Take your kids grocery shopping with you: Get your kids involved in shopping decisions. It may take a little more time in the supermarket but it could lead to more harmonious mealtimes.
- Keep junk food out of the house: Your kids can't eat unhealthy snacks if you don't buy them. Keep healthy foods on hand instead: 100 percent juice instead of colas or sugary drinks, and a bowl of fresh or dried fruit instead of chips.
- Repeal the "clean your plate" rule: Kids know when they're full, so let them stop. Overeating is one of the major reasons we get too many calories.
- Be a good role model: If your kids see you eating and enjoying a variety of healthy foods, they're more likely to try them too. If you refuse to eat certain foods how can you expect your kids to?

Mega Turkey Nacho Dinner

Just as for chicken fingers and Buffalo-style anything, you can't have too many recipes for nachos. These nachos are topped with lots of veggies and make a super-satisfying dinner. When it comes to cheese for my nachos—or the use of cheese in general—I prefer to use less of a good-quality, strongly flavored cheese rather than lots of reduced-fat, flat-flavored cheese.

INGREDIENTS

- 2 tablespoons EVOO (extra-virgin olive oil), twice around the pan
- 1 pound ground turkey breast
- 1 tablespoon chili powder, a palmful
- ½ tablespoon ground cumin, ½ palmful
- 1 onion, chopped
- 2 to 3 garlic cloves, chopped
- 1 large carrot, peeled and grated
- 1 small zucchini, ends trimmed, halved lengthwise, and sliced into half moons
  Salt and freshly ground black pepper
- 1 (4-ounce) can sliced green chiles, drained
- 1 (10-ounce) box frozen corn kernels
- 1 (15-ounce) can black beans, rinsed and drained
- ½ cup chicken stock
- ¼ cup fresh cilantro or flat-leaf parsley leaves, chopped
  Zest and juice of 1 lime
- 1 (9 to 13-ounce) bag multi-grain tortilla chips
- 1½ cups shredded pepper Jack or sharp Cheddar cheese
- 2 plum tomatoes, seeded and chopped
- 1 avocado, cut in half, pit removed, flesh removed and chopped

THE ITTY BITTIES CAN:

- peel carrot
- rinse and drain beans
- zest and juice lime
- grate cheese

Preheat the oven to 375°F.

Heat the EVOO in a large skillet over medium-high heat. Add the ground turkey and cook for 3 to 4 minutes, breaking it up with the back of a wooden spoon. Season with the chili powder and cumin. Add the onions, garlic, carrots, and zucchini and season with salt and pepper. Cook for 8 to 10 minutes, then stir in the chiles, corn, and beans and heat through. Adjust the seasonings. Stir in the chicken stock and cook for 1 to 2 minutes longer. Remove from the heat and stir in the cilantro, 1 teaspoon of the lime zest, and the lime juice.

Arrange one third of the bag of chips on a rimmed baking sheet, top with one third of the turkey-vegetable mixture, and sprinkle with one third of the cheese. Repeat 2 more times to make triple-decker stacks, ending with the cheese. Transfer to the oven and bake until the cheese is melted, 5 to 6 minutes. Top with the tomatoes and chopped avocado and serve.

SERVES 4

Antip-achos: Italian Nachos and Fish Stick Parm

INGREDIENTS

- 2 tablespoons EVOO (extra-virgin olive oil)
- 2 garlic cloves, grated
- Pinch of red pepper flakes
- 1 (15-ounce) can crushed tomatoes
- Salt and freshly ground black pepper
- 1 box organic frozen fish sticks (18 sticks)
- 1½ cups shredded Provolone cheese
- 1 cup grated Parmigiano-Reggiano cheese
- ½ cup shredded fresh basil, about 10 leaves
- 6 pita breads
- Olive oil cooking spray
- 1 teaspoon garlic powder
- 1 teaspoon dried thyme or oregano leaves
- 3 roasted red peppers, drained, patted dry, and chopped
- 1 small jar marinated mushrooms, drained and chopped
- 1 (15-ounce) can quartered artichoke hearts in water, drained
- ½ cup pitted good-quality olives, chopped

THE ITTY BITTIES CAN:

- shred basil leaves
- drain and chop roasted red peppers
- chop olives
- cut pita, arrange on baking sheet, and season

INSTRUCTIONS

Preheat the oven to 425°F.

Heat the EVOO in a small sauce pot over medium heat. Add the garlic and red pepper flakes and cook for a minute or two, then stir in the tomatoes and season with salt and pepper. Simmer for a few minutes.

Arrange the fish sticks in a 9 x 13-inch baking dish and pour half the tomato sauce over the fish, reserving the rest to pass at the dinner table. Scatter ½ cup of the Provolone cheese and the Parm over the fish and bake for 18 minutes, or until the fish is crispy and the cheese has melted. Garnish with the shredded basil.

While the fish bakes, cut the pita breads into wedges, 6 per pita, using a knife or kitchen scissors. Scatter the pita on a baking sheet, spray with olive oil cooking spray, and season with the garlic powder and dried thyme or oregano. Bake for 10 to 12 minutes or until crisp. Remove the baking pan from the oven and cover the pita chips with the roasted red peppers, mushrooms, artichokes, olives, and the remaining cup of Provolone cheese. Return the nachos to the oven for 5 minutes to melt the cheese, then serve along with the fish sticks.

SERVES 4

Lightened-Up Lemony Chinese Chicken

INGREDIENTS

- 3 cups **panko** (Japanese bread crumbs)
  Grated zest of 2 lemons
- 1 tablespoon **ground ginger**
- 2 tablespoons **sesame seeds**, a couple of palmfuls
  Salt and **freshly ground black pepper**
- 2 pounds **chicken tenders**
- ¼ cup **soy sauce** (eyeball it)
  Juice of 1 lemon
- 2 tablespoons **honey**
- 3 tablespoons chopped **fresh chives**

> **THE ITTY BITTIES CAN:**
> - zest lemons
> - combine bread-crumb mixture
> - shake chicken in bag

INSTRUCTIONS

Preheat the oven to 400°F.

Mix the panko, lemon zest, ground ginger, and sesame seeds in a 1-gallon plastic bag and mix well. Season with salt and pepper. Add the chicken a couple of pieces at a time and give them a good shake to coat. Arrange the coated pieces on a baking sheet. Repeat until all the chicken has been coated, then bake for 20 to 25 minutes.

In a small bowl whisk together the soy sauce, lemon juice, and honey with a little splash of water. Arrange the chicken on a plate, garnish with the chopped chives, and serve with the honey-soy-lemon dipping sauce on the side.

SERVES 4

lemon chicken with lemon rice

SUBMITTED BY KRISTINE B. AND HER SON NICHOLAS
(AGE NINE) FROM SALINAS, CALIFORNIA

KID 2 KID

Nick was brainstorming new ways to cook chicken again (and again and again . . .). Finding lemons, milk, and rice in the fridge, he came up with this recipe. Good job, Nick! Serve with steamed broccoli.

Zest and juice of 2 lemons • 4 boneless, skinless chicken breasts, halved crosswise • 2 garlic cloves, minced, divided • 3 tablespoons EVOO (extra-virgin olive oil) • Salt and freshly ground black pepper • 1½ cups long-grain rice • 3 cups chicken stock • 2 tablespoons all-purpose flour • 1 to 1½ cups milk

Sprinkle the zest and juice of 1 lemon over the chicken breasts. Add half of the minced garlic and 2 tablespoons of the EVOO. Sprinkle with salt and pepper and marinate for 15 to 30 minutes.

While the chicken marinates, combine the rice, chicken stock, and the juice of the second lemon in a saucepan and bring to a boil. Reduce the heat to a simmer, cover, and cook for 17 minutes, or until the rice is tender.

Heat the remaining tablespoon of EVOO in a large skillet. Remove the chicken from the marinade, reserving the marinade, and cook in the oil for 4 to 5 minutes on each side, or until golden and cooked through. Remove the chicken to a plate and cover loosely with foil to keep warm.

Pour the reserved marinade into the skillet and bring to a simmer. Add the flour and stir to make a roux. Gradually whisk in 1 to 1½ cups milk to make a medium-thick sauce. Return the chicken to the pan along with any juices on the plate and heat together for 2 to 3 minutes.

To serve, put some rice on a plate and add a chicken breast on top. Drizzle with some sauce and sprinkle with the remaining lemon zest.

SERVES 4

Sukiyaki Stir-fry

INGREDIENTS

- 1½ cups **brown rice**, cooked according to package directions
- 1½ pounds **beef sirloin**, 1 inch thick
- ⅓ cup **tamari** or soy sauce (eyeball it)
- ⅔ cup **beef stock** (eyeball it)
- 4 tablespoons **canola oil**
- 1 large **onion**, sliced
- ½ pound **shiitake mushrooms**, stemmed and sliced
- ½ pound **bok choy**, sliced (about 3 cups)
- 1 (4-ounce) can **bamboo shoots**, drained
- 4 **scallions**, thinly sliced on an angle
- 2 **egg yolks** or **1 rounded tablespoon cornstarch**

> **THE ITTY BITTIES CAN:**
> - stem and slice mushrooms
> - drain bamboo shoots

INSTRUCTIONS

Start the rice according to the package directions and place the meat in the freezer to firm up for slicing, 10 to 15 minutes.

When the rice is 10 to 15 minutes away from serving time, remove the meat from the freezer and slice it very thin, no more than ⅛ inch thick.

Combine the tamari and beef stock in a small saucepan and bring just to a simmer over low heat. Keep warm.

Heat about 2 tablespoons of the oil in a large nonstick skillet over high heat. When the oil smokes, stir-fry the meat to sear it, 4 to 5 minutes. Remove the meat from the pan and set aside. Add the remaining 2 tablespoons of oil to the skillet, then add the vegetables and stir-fry them for 3 to 4 minutes. Return the meat to the skillet.

In a small bowl, stir the yolks or cornstarch together with a little bit of the warm soy stock. Whisk the mixture into the saucepan with the remaining stock and stir over low heat until it thickens a bit. Pour the sauce over the stir fry, toss to combine, and serve immediately over the brown rice.

SERVES 4

Not-Fried Chicken on the Ranch and Peeler Salad

Here's an updated version of shake and bake–style chicken. The ranch dressing is made with buttermilk, which I always thought of as rich and fattening: NOT SO! Buttermilk is very low in fat because it is made from skim milk. This is one feel-good-about-it down-home supper.

INGREDIENTS

- 3 cups panko (Japanese bread crumbs)
- 1½ teaspoons paprika, ½ palmful
- 1½ teaspoons garlic powder, ½ palmful
- 1½ teaspoons onion powder, ½ palmful
- 1 whole chicken, cut into 10 serving pieces
  Salt and freshly ground black pepper
- 1 cup buttermilk
  Juice of ½ lemon
- 1 garlic clove, grated or finely chopped
  A few dashes of hot sauce
- 2 tablespoons fresh flat-leaf parsley, about 1 palmful, chopped
- 2 tablespoons fresh dill, about 1 palmful, chopped
- 2 tablespoons fresh chives, a small palmful, chopped
- ½ seedless cucumber
- 1 large or 2 medium carrots, peeled
- 2 celery ribs
- ½ pint grape tomatoes, halved
- 2 hearts of romaine, chopped

THE ITTY BITTIES CAN:

- combine bread-crumb mixture
- make cucumber ribbons
- peel carrots

Preheat the oven to 400°F.

Mix the panko, paprika, garlic powder, and onion powder in a shallow dish. Season the chicken pieces liberally with salt and pepper and toss to coat in the crumbs. Place the coated chicken on a baking sheet and bake for 40 to 45 minutes, or until cooked through.

While the chicken bakes, make the ranch dressing. Mix together the buttermilk, lemon juice, garlic, hot sauce, parsley, dill, and chives in a bowl. Season with salt and pepper. Refrigerate until ready to serve.

When you are ready to eat, use a vegetable peeler to cut long, thin ribbons of cucumber, carrots, and celery. Combine the tomatoes and lettuce in a salad bowl and toss with the vegetable shavings and half the dressing.

Serve the chicken with the salad alongside and pass the remaining dressing to dab on the chicken.

SERVES 4

Chicken Sausages with BBQ Butter Beans and Cheddar Cauliflower

INGREDIENTS

- 8 **chicken sausages**, casings pierced, any variety
- 3 tablespoons **EVOO** (extra-virgin olive oil)
  Salt
- 1 large head of **cauliflower**, cut into florets
- 2 tablespoons **butter**
- 2 tablespoons **all-purpose flour**
- 2 cups **whole milk**
- 2 cups grated **sharp white Cheddar cheese**
  Freshly ground black pepper
- ⅛ teaspoon freshly grated or **ground nutmeg**, or more to taste
- 1 medium **onion**, yellow or red, chopped
- 2 **garlic cloves**, chopped
- 2 (15-ounce) cans **butter beans**, drained
- 3 tablespoons **brown sugar**
- 3 tablespoons **red wine vinegar**
- 2 tablespoons **Worcestershire sauce**
- 1 cup **tomato sauce**
- 1 tablespoon **grill seasoning blend**, such as McCormick's Montreal Steak Seasoning

THE ITTY
BITTIES CAN:

- break cauli-flower into pieces
- grate cheese
- drain beans

Place the sausages in a skillet in 1 inch water with 1 tablespoon of the EVOO, once around the pan, and bring to a boil. Let the sausages cook uncovered over medium-high heat until the liquid evaporates and the casings crisp up, 10 to 15 minutes.

In a saucepan, bring 1 inch water to a simmer, salt it, and add the cauliflower. Cook until tender, about 10 minutes.

In a medium sauce pot, melt the butter over medium heat and whisk in the flour. Cook for 1 minute, then whisk in the milk and bring to a bubble. Thicken the sauce until it coats the back of a spoon, 5 to 6 minutes, then stir in the cheese in a figure-eight pattern with a wooden spoon and season the sauce with salt, pepper, and nutmeg to taste.

Heat a medium skillet over medium to medium-high heat with the remaining 2 tablespoons EVOO. When the oil is hot, add the onions and garlic and cook for 6 to 7 minutes. Add the beans and warm through. Combine the brown sugar, vinegar, Worcestershire, tomato sauce, and grill seasoning, then stir the mixture into the beans and combine. Simmer for 5 minutes more.

Drain the cauliflower and add to the cheese sauce to combine.

Serve 2 links of sausage with some beans and Cheddar cauliflower alongside.

SERVES 4

dinner time!

Orange-Soy Pork Chops with Applesauce, Roast Potatoes, and Green Beans

Another take on Peter Brady's favorite.

- 1½ pounds baby red-skin potatoes, halved
- 5 tablespoons EVOO (extra-virgin olive oil)
  Salt and freshly ground black pepper
- 1 pound green beans, trimmed and cut into 1½-inch pieces
- ¼ cup fresh flat-leaf parsley leaves, a generous handful, chopped
- 5 McIntosh, Honey Crisp, or Gala apples, peeled, cored, and diced
- 1 cup unfiltered, natural apple cider
- 3 tablespoons dark brown sugar
- 4 (1-inch-thick) boneless pork loin chops, 6 to 8 ounces each
  Zest and juice of 1 orange
- ¼ cup tamari or soy sauce

> THE ITTY BITTIES CAN:
>
> - halve potatoes and drizzle with oil
> - chop parsley
> - peel apples
> - zest and juice orange

INSTRUCTIONS

Preheat the oven to 400°F.

Place the potatoes on a baking sheet. Drizzle with 3 tablespoons of the EVOO and season with salt and pepper. Roast for 25 minutes. In the last 15 minutes of cooking time, add the green beans to the baking sheet with the potatoes, toss to combine, and return to the oven. Once the potatoes and beans are cooked, remove from the oven and sprinkle with the parsley.

While the potatoes roast, combine the apples, apple cider, and brown sugar in a medium pot over medium-high heat. Cook until the apples cook down to a chunky sauce, 10 to 12 minutes, stirring occasionally. If the sauce begins to spatter as it bubbles, reduce the heat a bit.

Preheat a large skillet over medium-high heat with the remaining 2 tablespoons of EVOO, twice around the pan. Season the chops with salt and pepper. Brown the chops for 4 minutes on each side or until the juices run clear.

In a shallow dish, combine 1 teaspoon of the orange zest, the orange juice, and the tamari. Add the sauce to the pork and cook

for 2 minutes, until the sauce has reduced. Serve the chops with some sauce drizzled on top and the applesauce and roasted potatoes and green beans alongside.

SERVES 4

Inside-Out Sausage Chops with Roasted Peppers

In this recipe, all the flavors of sweet Italian sausage—fennel, garlic, cheese—are combined with sweet smothered onions and piled on top of lean pork loin chops. My mom's simple roasted peppers seemed the right side for this meal. If you like sausage, pepper, and onion subs at the ballpark or street fair, this meal is for you!

INGREDIENTS

- 4 bell peppers (mix up the colors), seeded and thickly sliced
- 4½ tablespoons EVOO (extra-virgin olive oil)
- 3 garlic cloves, 1 crushed, 2 finely chopped or grated
- Salt and freshly ground black pepper
- 4 boneless pork loin chops, about 1½ inches thick
- 2 large onions, thinly sliced
- 1 teaspoon fennel seeds
- Red pepper flakes (optional)
- 2-ounce chunk of Parmigiano-Reggiano cheese

> **THE ITTY BITTIES CAN:**
> - toss bell peppers with seasonings
> - shave Parmesan cheese

INSTRUCTIONS

Preheat the oven to 400°F.

Place the bell peppers in a baking dish with 2 tablespoons of the EVOO, add the crushed clove of garlic, and toss to coat. Season the peppers liberally with salt and pepper and roast for 15 to 20 minutes, until tender and dark at the edges.

Season the chops with salt and pepper. Heat ½ tablespoon of the EVOO, a healthy drizzle, in an ovenproof skillet over medium-high to high heat. When the pan begins to smoke, add the chops and sear, browning them for 2 to 3 minutes on each side. Transfer the skillet to the oven and roast the chops for 10 to 12 minutes. Remove the chops from the oven and let stand for a couple of minutes to concentrate the juices.

While the chops cook, smother the onions. To a second skillet add the remaining 2 tablespoons EVOO and the onions and place over medium to medium-high heat. Season the onions with salt and pepper and toss in the fennel seeds and chopped garlic. If you like hot sausage, add red pepper flakes. Cover loosely with foil and pat the foil down over the onions, smothering them and trapping the juices as they cook. Toss the onions every 2 to 3 minutes and cook until tender, about 10 minutes.

Top each chop with a pile of onions and garnish with shaved Parm cheese, using your veggie peeler to make long, thin shavings. Pile some roasted peppers alongside and serve.

SERVES 4

Turkey–Jweet Potato Jhepherd's Pie and Cran-Applesauce Jundaes

INGREDIENTS

- 2 tablespoons EVOO (extra-virgin olive oil)
- 2 pounds ground turkey or ground turkey breast or chopped leftover turkey
  Salt and freshly ground black pepper
- 2 teaspoons poultry seasoning
- 2½ pounds sweet potatoes, peeled and cubed
- 1 large onion, chopped or grated
- 2 large carrots, peeled and grated
- 4 to 6 celery ribs from the heart, chopped
- 4 tablespoons (½ stick) butter
- 2 tablespoons all-purpose flour
- 2 cups turkey or chicken stock
  A few dashes of Worcestershire sauce
- 1 (10-ounce) box frozen peas
- ⅓ ripe banana (enough for 4 or 5 slices)
  A few dashes of hot sauce
- 2 cups shredded sharp yellow Cheddar cheese

> **THE ITTY BITTIEJ CAN:**
> - peel sweet potatoes
> - peel and grate carrots
> - slice banana
> - shred cheese
> - zest orange

CRAN-APPLESAUCE SUNDAES

- 1½ cups all-natural applesauce
- ½ cup good-quality whole-berry cranberry sauce, such as Ocean Spray (in tubs on the canned fruit aisle)
- 2 pinches of ground cinnamon

2	teaspoons grated orange zest
2	pints reduced-fat French vanilla ice cream
	Whipped cream, for garnish
2	tablespoons chopped toasted pecans, available on the baking aisle

INSTRUCTIONS

Preheat the oven to 425°F.

In a deep skillet or a Dutch oven heat the EVOO over high heat. Add the turkey and break it up with a wooden spoon; season with salt and pepper and the poultry seasoning.

Place the sweet potatoes in a medium pot, cover with cold water, cover the pot, bring to a boil, season with salt, and cook for 15 minutes, or until the potatoes are tender.

Add the onions, carrots, and celery to the turkey. Stir and cook for 5 minutes. While the vegetables are cooking, heat 2 tablespoons of the butter in a small pot over medium heat. Add the flour to the melted butter and whisk for 1 minute, then whisk in the stock and season with salt, pepper, and the Worcestershire. Cook for a few minutes to thicken.

Stir the peas into the meat mixture and turn the heat off.

Drain the potatoes and return the pot to the heat. Add the remaining 2 table-spoons butter and melt over medium heat. Peel and slice the banana and add it with the potatoes to the pot. Season with salt, pepper, and the hot sauce. Mash the potatoes and banana to combine; adjust the seasoning. Top the meat mixture with the potato mixture. Cover the potatoes with the cheese and set in the oven. Bake to melt the cheese, about 5 minutes.

For dessert, warm the applesauce and cranberry sauce in the microwave or in a small pot over low heat and season with the cinnamon and orange zest. Place a little cran-applesauce in the bottom of a sundae dish, top with 2 scoops ice cream, add more sauce, and garnish with a small dollop of whipped cream. Sprinkle with a few chopped pecans.

SERVES 4 TO 6

These menus are all based on the back-in-the-day idea of a good, square meal: meat, vegetable, and starch. The flavors have all gotten an update, though!

No-Thyme Quick Chicken with Smash Broc-o-tatoes and Gouda Gravy

INGREDIENTS

- 4 **Idaho potatoes**, peeled and cut in 2-inch cubes
  Salt
- 4 (6-ounce) **boneless, skinless chicken breasts**
- 2 tablespoons chopped **fresh thyme** leaves
  Freshly ground black pepper
- 2 tablespoons **EVOO** (extra-virgin olive oil)
- 1 head of **broccoli**, trimmed and cut into florets and 1-inch cubes
- 2 tablespoons **butter**
- 2 tablespoons **all-purpose flour**
- 1 cup **chicken stock**
- 1½ cups **milk** or half-and-half
- 1½ cups shredded **Gouda cheese**

> **THE ITTY BITTIES CAN:**
> - peel potatoes
> - strip thyme leaves
> - grate cheese

INSTRUCTIONS

Place the potatoes in a large pot and cover with cold water. Bring to a boil, salt the water, reduce the heat a bit, and cook until tender, about 12 minutes. Heads-up: about halfway through you will add the broccoli to the pot, so use a pot large enough to accommodate both.

Season the chicken breasts with the thyme, salt, and pepper. Heat the EVOO in a skillet over medium-high heat and cook the chicken for 6 minutes on each side.

Add the broccoli to the potatoes and cook for 6 minutes.

Heat the butter in a small sauce pot over medium heat. When the butter has melted, add the flour and cook for 1 minute, then whisk in the chicken stock and 1 cup of the milk or half-and-half. Thicken for 2 to 3 minutes, season the sauce with salt and pepper, then stir in the cheese in a figure-eight motion with a wooden spoon for 2 minutes, or until the cheese is melted. Turn off the heat.

Drain the cooked broccoli and potatoes and return to the hot pot to dry them out. Mash the broccoli and potatoes together, using the remaining milk to reach the desired consistency. Season with salt and pepper.

Slice the chicken breasts on an angle. Pile some mashed broc-o-tatoes on plates and arrange the fanned-out chicken on the edge of the mound. Pour the Gouda gravy over the top.

SERVES 4

Chicken with Apple Gravy, Cheesy Rice Pilaf with Peas, and Green Beans with Scallions

INGREDIENTS

2	tablespoons **EVOO** (extra-virgin olive oil)
1½	cups **long-grain rice**
3½	cups **chicken stock**
4	boneless, skinless **chicken breasts**
2	tablespoons **butter**
1	tablespoon **all-purpose flour**
½	cup unfiltered, natural **apple cider**
	Salt and **freshly ground black pepper**
1	pound **green beans**, trimmed
2	**scallions**, white and green parts, chopped
1	cup **frozen peas**
¾	cup grated **sharp white Cheddar cheese**

> **THE ITTY BITTIES CAN:**
>
> - trim beans
> - grate cheese
> - stir in peas and cheese

INSTRUCTIONS

Pour 1 tablespoon of the EVOO into a sauce pot over medium heat, add the rice, and toast until the rice is light brown in color, 3 to 4 minutes. Stir in 2½ cups of the stock, bring to a boil, reduce the heat to medium-low, cover and cook for 16 to 18 minutes, or until the rice is tender.

While the rice cooks, heat the remaining tablespoon of EVOO in a skillet over medium-high heat. Cook the chicken breasts for 10 to 12 minutes, 5 to 6 minutes on each side, until the juices run clear; remove to a plate. Cover the chicken with foil. Add 1 tablespoon of the butter to the skillet, sprinkle in the flour, and cook for 1 minute. Whisk in the apple cider and 1 cup of the chicken stock, cook for about a minute to thicken the gravy, and season with salt and pepper. Turn off the heat.

While the chicken cooks, bring 1 inch water to a boil in a saucepan. Add salt and the green beans, cover, and cook for 3 to 4 minutes or to desired doneness. Drain the beans, return them to the hot pan, and toss with the remaining tablespoon of butter, cut into small pieces, and the scallions. Season with salt and pepper.

In the last 2 to 3 minutes of the rice's cooking time, stir in the peas and cheese.

Serve the rice and beans alongside the chicken breasts and pour the apple gravy over the chicken.

SERVES 4

chili lime chicken

SUBMITTED BY KAREN K. AND HER DAUGHTER ROSE
(AGE FIFTEEN) FROM CINCINNATI, OHIO

KID 2 KID

Serve with a black bean and corn salad.

4 to 6 boneless, skinless chicken breasts • 1 garlic clove, minced • 2 tablespoons chili powder • 1½ tablespoons ground cumin • Hot sauce • 1 lime, zested and halved • EVOO (extra-virgin olive oil) • Salt and freshly ground black pepper

Rinse the chicken breasts and pierce them a few times on each side with a fork. In a resealable plastic bag combine the garlic, chili powder, cumin, hot sauce to taste, and lime zest. Drizzle some EVOO into the bag and season with salt and pepper. Add the chicken, seal the bag, and shake to distribute the marinade. Refrigerate for 30 minutes to 2 hours.

Preheat barbecue grill or ridged grill pan.

Grill the chicken for 6 to 7 minutes per side, or until cooked through. Transfer to a platter and squeeze the lime juice on top.

SERVES 4 TO 6

Pork Chops, Golden Apple and Raisin Sauce, and Whole-Wheat Pasta Mac-n-Cheddar with Broccoli

Salt

½ pound whole-wheat penne

4 golden apples, cored and chopped

1 cup unfiltered, natural apple cider

3 tablespoons brown sugar

A handful of golden raisins

1 teaspoon ground cinnamon

4 large center-cut pork loin chops, 1½ inches thick

Black pepper

2 tablespoons EVOO (extra-virgin olive oil)

2 tablespoons butter

1 rounded tablespoon all-purpose flour

1½ cups milk

½ pound extra-sharp white Cheddar cheese, grated

Freshly grated or ground nutmeg

2 cups broccoli tops, cut into small florets

2 tablespoons spicy brown or grainy Dijon mustard

¼ cup pure maple syrup

THE ITTY BITTIES CAN:

- cut broccoli into florets
- grate cheese

INSTRUCTIONS

Bring a large pot of water to a boil over high heat for the pasta. Season the water with salt and cook the pasta al dente.

While the water is heating, add the apples to a medium pot and stir in the cider, brown sugar, raisins, and cinnamon. Place the pot over medium-high heat and cook until the apples are tender, about 12 minutes.

Season the chops with salt and pepper. Heat the EVOO in a skillet over medium-high heat. Add the chops and cook for 6 to 7 minutes on each side.

While the chops cook, heat the butter in a sauce pot over medium heat. Whisk in the flour and cook for 1 minute, then whisk in the milk and season with salt and pepper. Stir the cheese into the sauce and season with nutmeg to taste. Reduce the heat to low.

Add the broccoli to the pasta during the last 2 minutes of cooking time. Drain and return to the pasta pot. Add the cheese sauce and stir to coat.

Add the mustard and maple syrup to the chops and cook until a glaze forms, about 1 minute. Spoon the glaze over the chops.

Serve the pork with the apple sauce, and with the mac-n-Cheddar with broccoli alongside.

SERVES 4, WITH LEFTOVER MAC FOR SNACK-ATTACKS!

Paprika Pork Cutlets with Swiss Chard Egg Noodles

- 4 (6-ounce) boneless pork loin chops
  Salt and freshly ground black pepper
- 1 cup all-purpose flour
- 1 teaspoon smoked paprika
- 2 eggs, beaten
- 1 cup plain bread crumbs
- ¼ cup canola or vegetable oil
- 2 tablespoons butter
- 1 bunch of Swiss chard, deveined and chopped
- ½ pound extra-wide egg noodles
  Freshly grated or ground nutmeg
- 4 lemon wedges

THE ITTY BITTIES CAN:

- pound and bread pork chops
- beat eggs

INSTRUCTIONS

Place a large pot of water on to boil for the egg noodles.

Place the chops between wax paper or plastic wrap and pound out no more than ¼ inch thick. Season the pork cutlets with salt and pepper. Combine the flour and paprika on a plate. Beat the eggs in a shallow dish. Place the bread crumbs on a second plate. Coat the chops in flour, shake off the excess, then coat them in egg and bread crumbs.

Heat about 3 tablespoons of the oil in a large skillet over medium-high heat. When hot, add the cutlets and cook until golden, about 4 minutes on each side.

Heat the remaining 1 tablespoon oil and the butter in a deep skillet over medium heat. When the butter melts into the oil, add the chard and cook for 6 to 7 minutes. Drop the egg noodles into the pot of boiling, salted water after a minute or two. When the noddles are al dente, drain and add to the chard, toss, and season with salt, pepper, and nutmeg to taste.

Serve the cutlets with Swiss chard and noodles and lemon wedges.

SERVES 4

Spicy Spanish Shrimp, Cheesy Orzo, and Roasted Green Beans

- 1¼ pounds green beans, trimmed of stem ends
- 3 tablespoons EVOO (extra-virgin olive oil)
  Salt and freshly ground black pepper
- ½ pound orzo
- ¼ pound chorizo or other spicy sausage, diced
- 1 onion, chopped
- 1 red bell pepper, seeded and chopped
- 1 small jalapeño pepper, seeded and finely chopped
- 1 garlic clove, chopped
- 1 pound large shrimp, peeled and deveined
- 1 teaspoon smoked regular or sweet paprika
- 1 (15-ounce) can diced tomatoes
- 1 cup grated or shredded Manchego cheese or other tangy white cheese
  A handful of fresh flat-leaf parsley, finely chopped

> THE ITTY BITTIES CAN:
> - trim beans
> - grate cheese
> - chop parsley

INSTRUCTIONS

Bring a large pot of water to a boil for the orzo.

Preheat the oven to 400°F.

When the oven is hot, pile the green beans on a rimmed baking sheet. Toss the beans with 2 tablespoons of the EVOO to coat and season with salt and pepper. Roast for 15 minutes, or until brown at the edges and tender.

When the water comes to a boil, salt it and cook the orzo al dente.

Heat the remaining tablespoon of EVOO in a deep, large skillet over medium-high heat. Add the chorizo and render it for 1 minute, then add the onions, peppers, and garlic and season with salt and pepper. Cook the vegetables for 5 minutes, then season the shrimp with the paprika and toss into the pan. Stir in the tomatoes and cook for 5 minutes, or until the shrimp are pink and firm.

Drain the pasta and place it in a medium bowl. Stir in the cheese and parsley to evenly coat the orzo.

Serve the shrimp alongside the orzo and roasted green beans.

SERVES 4

Almond Snapper Fillets, Herb Rice with Peas and Carrots

1¾ cups **chicken stock**

2 tablespoons **butter**

1 cup **long-grain rice**

2 **carrots**, peeled and chopped or shredded

1 cup **frozen peas**

3 **scallions**, white and green parts, finely chopped

3 tablespoons **fresh dill**, chopped

A handful of **fresh flat-leaf parsley**, finely chopped

¼ cup slivered or sliced **almonds**

1 tablespoon **EVOO** (extra-virgin olive oil)

4 (5- to 6-ounce) **red snapper fillets**

Salt and **freshly ground black pepper**

All-purpose flour, for dusting

Juice of ½ lemon

> ### THE ITTY BITTIES CAN:
> - peel carrots
> - chop dill and parsley
> - dust fillets with flour

Heat the stock and 1 tablespoon of the butter in a large pot until boiling. Stir in the rice and carrots and cover the pot. Simmer for 12 to 13 minutes, then stir in the peas and scallions and cook for 3 to 4 minutes more. Turn off the heat and fluff the rice with a fork. Stir in the dill and parsley.

While the rice cooks, toast the nuts in a large skillet until golden, 5 to 6 minutes over medium heat. Remove the nuts and reserve. Add the EVOO and the remaining tablespoon of butter to the skillet. Season the fish with salt and pepper and dust it lightly in flour. Cook the fish for 3 to 4 minutes on each side, until golden and firm. Squeeze the lemon juice over them in the pan.

Serve the fish with lots of nuts on top and with the veggie-herb rice alongside.

baked grouper with roasted asparagus

SUBMITTED BY MALORI M. AND HER DAUGHTER KALLIE (AGE FIFTEEN) FROM FORT WORTH, TEXAS

4 tablespoons melted butter • Juice of 1 lemon • 1 teaspoon paprika • 1 teaspoon garlic powder • Salt and freshly ground black pepper • ¼ cup chopped fresh flat-leaf parsley • 2 (6-ounce) grouper fillets • ½ bunch of asparagus, trimmed

Preheat the oven to 400°F.

In a small bowl, stir together the butter and lemon juice. In a separate small bowl, mix the paprika, garlic powder, salt and pepper, and parsley. Add enough of the lemon butter to make a paste. Spread the paste evenly over both sides of the grouper fillets. Arrange the fillets and the asparagus on a baking sheet and roast for 10 to 15 minutes, or until the fish is cooked through and the asparagus is nice and tender.

SERVES 2

CornFlake-Crusted Tilapia with Sweet and Spicy Watermelon Salsa

One sunny afternoon at the Central Park Zoo I went head-to-head with a zoologist in a cook-off for the resident polar bears. The bears loved my meal and I won the throw down! If the polar bears like it, I bet the kids will, too! I have modified the recipe a bit. For the bears I left the fish whole—head and all. Otherwise, the ingredients are pretty much the same: watermelon, peppers, cereal, fish. Sounds weird, but it really is yum-o!

INGREDIENTS

- ½ small **seedless watermelon**, rind removed, flesh cut in ½-inch dice
- ½ **green bell pepper**, seeded and chopped
- ½ small **red onion**, chopped
- 1 **jalapeño pepper**, seeded and finely chopped
  Juice of 1 lime
  Salt and **freshly ground black pepper**
- 2 cups **cornflake crumbs** (eyeball it)
- 1 teaspoon **dry mustard**, ⅓ palmful
- ½ tablespoon **ground coriander**, ½ palmful
- ½ tablespoon **paprika**, ½ palmful
- 4 **tilapia fillets**
- 2 tablespoons **EVOO** (extra-virgin olive oil), twice around the pan

> **THE ITTY BITTIES CAN:**
>
> - cube watermelon
> - crush cornflakes
> - coat fillets

In a bowl combine the watermelon, bell pepper, onion, jalapeño, and lime juice. Season with a little salt and pepper, stir to combine, and reserve.

In a shallow dish, combine the cornflake crumbs, dry mustard, coriander, and paprika. Season the tilapia fillets with salt and pepper, then coat them thoroughly in the seasoned cornflake crumbs. Preheat a large nonstick skillet with the EVOO over medium-high heat. Once the oil starts to ripple, add the tilapia and cook for 3 to 4 minutes on each side, or until cooked through.

Top the fish with some of the watermelon salsa and serve.

SERVES 4

AFTERWORD
from the Alliance for a Healthier Generation

Helping your kids get and stay healthy isn't always easy, but preparing meals together is a great start in the right direction.

The best way to help our children become healthier is to help THEM take charge of their own health. You can influence what your kids eat, where they eat, and encourage them to play and exercise more. You may not be able to control everything, but by making healthy choices when and where you can, you'll start to see some positive changes.

As parents, you are the most important influence in your kids' lives. That's why the Alliance for a Healthier Generation is working with Yum-o!, and we've got lots of free tools to help you! Visit www.healthiergeneration.org to learn more.

Oh, and don't forget—encourage your kids to pledge to Go Healthy at www.igohugo.org, where they can join thousands of other kids who are pushing (and pulling and tugging and running and bending) to get active, eat better and have fun.

ACKNOWLEDGMENTS

Thank you to everyone who is checking out our Yum-o! website and getting involved; teachers and parents who are encouraging healthy lifestyles; and to Kappy and Roe and everyone who works on Yum-o!

Thanks to my family for making the kitchen the most important room in our house and for teaching me that good food provides you with a great life. Thanks to our terrific food team: Emily and the kids in the kitchen (Abby, Kara, and Patrick) who are always coming up with cute snacks. Thanks to my right and left hand, Michelle Boxer.

This book wouldn't look as gorgeous as it does without the help of designer Jenny Beal. Of course, thanks to Pam Krauss and Amy Boorstein; these ladies really know how to get the job done—fast!

And lastly, thanks to Katie Workman and Gary, Jack, and Charlie Freilich; Marysarah Quinn and Katie, Dylan, and Mark Garafalo; Adrian, Rica, and Cyrille Allannic; Jeremy Allen; Suzanne Gluck and Kaye and Nick Dyja; Marykay Pavol and Riley, Ava, and Doug Jones; Rhea, Maxwell, Tracy, and Anthony McFarlane; Phoebe Bradford; Monty, Michelle, and Adam Boxer; Claire, Janet, and Frank Annino; Madeline, Meeri, and Steve Cunniff; Eric Martin and Veda Carey-Martin; and my photo team, Alexandra Grablewski and Megan Schlow.

Index

Note: *Italicized* page references indicate photographs.

224